Footplate Memories
and Personal
Reminiscences

YEOVIL TO TAUNTON

Via Martock, Langport West and Durston

Derek Phillips

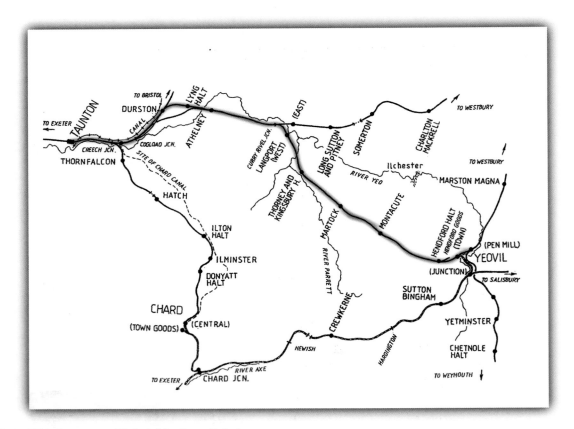

Set in Times New Roman and Printed in Great Britain
By Flaydemouse, Pen Mill Trading Estate, 8 Buckland Road, Yeovil, Somerset BA21 5EA

ISBN 0-9553334-0-7
      978-0-9553334-0-8

British Library Cataloguing Publication Data: a Catalogue for this book is available from the British Library

© Derek Phillips 2006

First published in 2006 by
Footplate Publishing Ltd. 4 White Mead. Yeovil. Somerset. BA21 3RX

Acknowledgements
I would like to thank everyone for their memories, photographs or at times just jogging my memory when putting together this book; John Cornelius, Mike Herrin, Clarence John Bradley, Malcolm Evans, John Day, Pam White, Jill Clark, Patrick Palmer, Alec Bowditch, Lens of Sutton, The Transport Treasury, R.S.Carpenter, Rothbury Press, Colin Hayward, Mike King, South Western Circle, Paul Chancellor, H.B.Priestley, H.M.R.S. University of Reading, Peter Barnfield, Pam Rayne, C.L.Caddy, R.E.Toop, P.J.Garland Collection, Alec Swain, Nicholas Chipchase, Western Gazette, Western Daily Press, Jim Cole, Wyndham Palmer.

Front Cover picture: 61XX 2-6-2T.6146 departs from Thorney & Kingsbury Halt with the 12.50 Taunton-Yeovil on
                      25 January 1962.   *John Cornelius*
Title Page picture: Battle of Britain class 4-6-2 No.34084 *253 Squadron* arrives at Yeovil Town from Yeovil Junction on
                      28 October 1961.   *John Cornelius*
Back Cover picture: 45XX 2-6-2T No.5504 with a Taunton train at Yeovil Town c1960   *Geoff Warnes/Colour-rail*

CONTENTS

FOOTPLATE MEMORIES
AND
PERSONAL REMININSCENCES

YEOVIL TO TAUNTON
Via Martock, Langport West and Durston

Derek Phillips

Introduction

The opening of the Bristol and Exeter Railway broad-gauge line from Durston to a station situated at Hendford on the outskirts of Yeovil on 1st October 1853 placed the town on the railway map.

A second broad-gauge railway appeared at Yeovil on 1st September 1856 when the Great Western railway opened the line between Frome and Pen Mill Station; connection to Weymouth was accomplished in January of the following year. The Salisbury and Yeovil Railway a standard-gauge line operated by the L&SWR appeared at Yeovil on 1st June 1860.

My own memories of the branch line to Taunton, apart from boyhood memories, stem from my firing days at Yeovil Town Locomotive Shed during the early 1960s.

Most of my footplate life was spent working on locomotives between Salisbury and Exeter Central where all trains (including freight) ran to a tightly timed schedule under the auspices of the Southern Region. However our shed also worked passenger trains over the old GWR route to Taunton, this was a typical branch line, and although trains ran to a timed schedule, there was a more relaxed air, almost like being in a different world.

Imagine what it was like, when the line eastwards from Montacute ran through a cutting. A haven for wildlife during the long gaps between trains, a rustle in the undergrowth, as a fox emerges, sniffs the air cautiously and then bounds across the railway track disappearing into the vegetation as quickly as it had arrived. The beautiful song of a blackbird merges with the harsh call of the magpie. Butterflies and bees dart amongst the flower and fauna in the hot sunshine.

England in high summer – there is no other place in the world like it.

In the distance can be heard the sound of a train leaving Montacute station, a faint blast on the whistle, the exhaust beat of the locomotive growing stronger and louder as it nears the overbridges at the top of the bank. The gleaming rails quiver under the approaching weight of a pannier tank hauling a two-coach B set coughing its way past the summit and onwards to Yeovil. Leaving a trail of steam and smoke in its wake. The cutting once again lapsing into silence, broken only by the birdsong and the occasional distant hum of a tractor in a nearby field.

Only the two beautiful bridges built by the Bristol and Exeter Railway to encompass its broad-gauge track, remain as testament to what many consider to have been the golden age of railways. Sadly the bridges now look down upon the busy A3088 link road from Cartgate roundabout on the A303 to Yeovil which has been built upon the trackbed that once ran through Montacute.

The old branch line and its stations has now faded into history, but as long as the memories remain with us, we who were fortunate to know the line, either as railway staff, or as passengers – then the line will never die.

Of such things, are dreams and memories made. Never forgotten.

Derek Phillips
Yeovil
2006

2-6-2T 6157 arrives at Martock with a Taunton-Yeovil train on 28 April 1962.

P.J. Garland Collection

41206 and 41305 run around their train at Yeovil Town station on 20 September 1964 after arrival from Yeovil Junction with the S.C.T.S. Farewell to Steam Railtour.　　　　*Alec Swain/Transport Treasury*

Class 4MT 2-6-0 No. 76005 stands on the No.3 road at Yeovil Town shed on 20 September 1964.
Alec Swain/Transport Treasury

The frontage of Yeovil Town shed on 15 September 1949 with from left to right L11 No.412 alongside the coaling platform on shed road 1, S15 829 is having smokebox char removed on No.2 road and L11 No.134 on No.3 road

A.E.West

Yeovil Town footplate staff Bob Hayward, Vic Burt and George Norris pose on the framing of T9 4-4-0 No.710 in the late 1940's.

Colin Hayward

No.34069 *Hawkinge* stands in the locomotive sidings at Yeovil Town. Note the A35 van near the parcels shed, collectors item nowadays.
Paul Chancellor Collection

The rear of Yeovil Town shed with locomotives standing on what was known as the 'table' road with K10 No.340 in the foreground on 30 March 1948.

A.E.West

45xx 2-6-2T No.4593 stands outside the shed on No.3 road on 9 June 1963. Debris of a working loco shed is strewn around in the foreground, discarded fire irons, baffle plate and a shovel lie in wait to trip the unwary.

Paul Chancellor Collection

Class V 4-4-0 No. 30902 *Wellington* stands at the end of the coal road at Yeovil Town on 29 September 1961. She will work the 4.06pm Yeovil Town to Salisbury crewed by Salisbury men.

A.E.West

The crew of S453 *King Arthur* pose for the camera at Yeovil town shed in the late 1940s.

Paul Chancellor Collection

Class U 2-6-0 31798 with tail lamp in position on the front buffer-beam leaves the shed at Yeovil Town before reversing to Yeovil Junction on 28 October 1961.

John Cornelius

Class O2 0-4-4T 30182 stands on the table road at Yeovil Town on 15 May 1954, this loco is equipped with Westinghouse equipment for working the push & pull services between the Town and Junction stations.

Paul Chancellor Collection

A scene full of sadness at Yeovil Town shed in March 1968, tracks and platforms have been demolished, and access to Yeovil Junction is now via Pen Mill station. D870 *Zulu* stands on No.3 shed road.

John Cornelius

Yeovil Town breakdown train coach DS 1588 in the shed yard on 29 September 1961, painted dark grey this is a former L&SWR brake 3rd.

A.E.West

Fred Martin pictured here on 5565 at Yeovil Pen Mill, as I will always remember him, full of good humour, and an excellent engine driver.   *Fred Martin*

Yeovil Pen Mill locomotive shed and turntable with a lone pannier tank in attendance, as viewed from Wyndham Hill.

Lens of Sutton Association

The branch line to Yeovil Town is seen in the foreground with Pen Mill locomotive shed beyond on 29 July 1951. A pannier tank stands near to the turntable next to the ash truck and breakdown van, another pannier stands in front of the shed building. *Lens of Sutton Association*

2-6-2T No.82040 shunts the down yard at Yeovil Pen Mill on 20 April 1964 after working over the branch from Taunton with the 6.45am passenger train under Taunton Duty No.33. The loco is booked to shunt at Pen Mill from 8.00-8.45am, plus a trip to Yeovil Town and return, before departing with the 9.56am passenger to Taunton. *John Cornelius*

Yeovil Pen Mill station in 1950. The curve in the up main line to the left is seen to good effect, compared with the dead straight down main line to the right of the island platform. Wagons await collection in the down yard, the signal box and goods shed can be seen in the distance.

R.S.Carpenter/A.W.V Mace Collection.

Yeovil Pen Mill looking east, a Weymouth train headed by a Bulldog 4-4-0 stands alongside the down platform. The overall roof was removed in 1934. The station opened on 1 September 1856 and celebrates its 150th Anniversary in 2006.

Authors Collection

A view underneath the original wooden overall roof at Yeovil Pen Mill Station pre 1934. Passengers and staff pose for the camera on the up platform, boxes of Yeovil made gloves are stacked on the trolley awaiting the next train. Note the station sign informing passengers to 'change for Durston Branch'. The footbridge at the far end of the platforms is still in use in 2006.

Authors Collection

Yeovil Pen Mill 13 August 1958 with Castle Class No.7014 *Caerhays Castle* on the left with a Weymouth train, the points are in the favour of 5543 awaiting departure for Taunton, 5563 is seen on shed in the distance.   *H.B.Priestley*

28XX 2-8-0 No.3819 stands underneath the A30 roadbridge at Pen Mill station whilst shunting the down yard, before resuming its journey with a Bristol to Weymouth freight train on 27 June 1961. The 10mph-speed restriction to the left refers to the curve through the up platform.   *John Day*

Pen Mill station looking east from the up platform, showing the water column at the end of the down platform on the right. Spare 'B' set coaches, used on the Taunton branch, stand in the bay to the left.

H.B.Priestley

Looking westwards from the up platform at Pen Mill with the rear of a Taunton bound train in the station.

Lens of Sutton Association

Coaches for a Yeovil to Weymouth excursion are being shunted in the down yard by 31791 on 4 September 1959. A DMU in 'cats whisker' livery has arrived with a Weymouth – Bristol train at the up platform.

H.B.Priestley

Coaching stock used on local trains to Taunton and Weymouth are stabled either side of the up main line as D7000 prepares to leave with the 3.10pm Weymouth to Bristol on 1 October 1961.

John Day

Hymek D7054 stands alongside the down platform at Pen Mill with the 9.15am Swindon – Weymouth parcel train on 21 March 1964. No.82044 steam heats its train in the down yard, before returning to Taunton.

John Day

No.5529 heads bunker-first from Pen Mill for Yeovil Town with a Taunton train in 1951.

R.S.Carpenter

Yeovil Town station and the L&SWR engine shed in July 1886. The overall roofs of the station contained 15,000 sq. ft of glass supported on iron pillars. A Beyer Peacock 0-6-0 single framed goods engine stands in the loco yard.

Authors Collection

The station frontage of Yeovil Town station in 1886 designed in the Tudor style by Sir William Tite architect of the original Nine Elms terminus and many station buildings on the LSWR Salisbury to Exeter line. The building on the left with the lamp is the Alexandra Hotel still trading in 2006.

Authors Collection

A classic view taken of Yeovil Town locomotive shed from Summerhouse Hill on 12 April 1925. Drummond locomotives, ex LSWR coaching stock and the overall glass roofs all compliment the scene.
Authors Collection

5542 approaches Yeovil Town off the branch line from Pen Mill with a Taunton train in 1950.

R.S.Carpenter/A.W.V Mace Collection

With the steam sanding gear being applied to assist adhesion. No.34023 *Blackmore Vale* departs from Yeovil Town with the 7.45am to Ilfracombe on 1 July 1961,

John Cornelius

Passengers move forward at Yeovil Town as a train for Taunton arrives during the 1950s. The double-track branch line to Yeovil Junction is on the right.   *R.S.Carpenter*

Drummond M7 0-4-4T No.30131 with tail lamp on the buffer beam, waits to propel its push & pull stock to Yeovil Junction on 22 August 1959. Trains for Yeovil Junction could depart for the junction station from any of the three platforms at Yeovil Town.   *A.E.West*

The railway shunting horse looks on nonchalantly as railway staff prepare to push a 12 ton rectangular tar wagon off the wagon turntable in Yeovil Town goods yard and across Dodham Lane into the gas works to the left on 13 August 1946, this area is now occupied by Somerfields Supermarket and car park. *A.E.West*

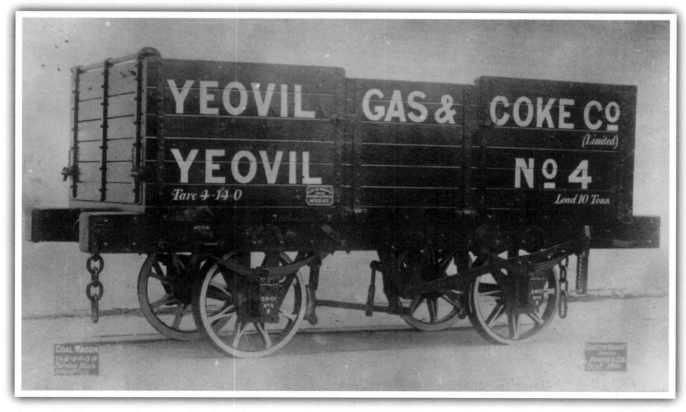

A works photograph taken by the Gloucester Railway Carriage & Wagon Company in September 1886 of a wagon built for the Yeovil Gas & Coke Ltd, painted black with white lettering the wagon is fitted with dumb buffers and early type link coupling.
HMRS/Glos.C&W

An 8-ton truck used by W.C.Clarke, Merchant, Yeovil in 1886, the wagon is in black livery with white lettering, dumb buffers are typical of the period.

HMRS/Glos.C&W

A Somerset Trading Company Ltd, Yeovil, 8-ton truck, photographed in June 1904 in bright red livery with white lettering, shaded black.

HMRS/Glos.C&W

Wagon belonging to the Yeovil Gas works in October 1912, the 10-ton wagon was painted chocolate, with white lettering shaded black.

HMRS/Glos.C&W

Pannier tank 0-6-0 No.5798 leaves Yeovil Town for Taunton with a mixed goods train on 28 October 1961. Most of the complement of wagons will be shunted off at Hendford Goods.

John Cornelius

King Arthur Class 4-6-0 No.30798 *Sir Hectimere* reverses into the goods shed siding at Yeovil Town on 25 January 1962, tanneries and glove factories stand alongside the railway. The line to the right in front of the locomotive is the branch line to Hendford and Taunton.

John Day

L11 4-4-0 No.163 known to footplatemen as a 'Large Hopper' stands in the goods shed siding at Yeovil Town on 13 August 1946. Locomotives were not allowed through the goods shed. The goods yard beyond was at right angles to the station, freight stock used wagon turntables, and were shunted originally by horses until replacement by a tractor fitted with a buffer beam.   *A.E.West*

One month before closure to passenger traffic, 2-6-2T No.4591 arrives at Hendford with the 12.37 Yeovil Pen Mill to Taunton on 16 May 1964, the locomotive and train are passing over Hendford Goods Junction.

John Day

YEOVIL TOWN LOCOMOTIVE SHED

I had started at Yeovil Town shed in the traditional way as an engine cleaner in 1957 and found myself in a working environment unlike any other as I in company with all of the other shed cleaners, became involved in duties, which not only comprised cleaning locomotives but also a myriad of tasks such as ensuring plenty of dried sand was available for the locomotives from the sand furnace, assisting the coalmen during busy periods, taking duty slips around the town to the houses of drivers and fireman who were off duty, cleaning the drivers cabin, helping the shed staff, lifting and shifting bricks for the brick arches in locomotives under repair, as well as having to assist the locomotive fitters at times with lifting springs, brake blocks etc, it was considered fair game by all of the shed staff to use engine cleaners for all tasks imaginable, after all we were on the lowest rung of the footplate ladder. But for all that it was a happy shed to work in and a great bunch of blokes to work with.

However in common with all engine cleaners working in sheds everywhere I progressed to the position of passed cleaner and then eventual promotion to fireman working on freight and passenger trains along the Southern Region main line between Salisbury and Exeter.

All types of locomotives became my 'bread and butter' at all hours of the day and night including our own Yeovil allocated U Class 2-6-0 tender engines known to all crews as 'rivers' a popular type of engine to work on, all Southern Region footplatemen knew that a good 'river' was worth its weight in gold, a very popular and free steaming class of locomotive, approximately 15 locomotives were stabled at the shed in my firing days, Bulleid Pacific's etc were not stabled here, but worked in on a daily basis from other Southern sheds. The legendary King Arthur class were also popular, as were the S15 4-6-0's Drummond T9s and the M7 tanks used on the branch services between Yeovil Town and Yeovil Junction stations.

The favourite class of all to work on had to be the Bulleid Pacifics. Superb runners and free steaming machines, I have had many good trips on them. The unrebuilt versions of both the West Country and Battle of Britain classes were all known as 'West Country's and the rebuilt versions as packet's.

The small ex GWR locomotive shed at Yeovil Pen Mill which had been under the control of the Southern Region since 1958, closed on 5 January 1959 with the crews, plus pannier Tanks. 3671, 3733, 4656, 8745, 9732, 9764 & 2-6-2 prairie tanks 5548 and 5563 transferred to our shed at the town, this also included the Western Region work and swelled our duties to include working passenger trains on the branch to Taunton, shunting at Hendford Goods, banking trains on the Evershot bank from Yetminster on the Yeovil – Weymouth main line, banking engines at night between Castle Cary and Witham and a night freight from Hendford Goods to Westbury and return.

The enginemens cabin was extended to cope with the extra staff, and a new water tank erected at the rear of the shed, replacing the old 'South Western' tank that ran inside the length of the shed over the fitters workshop and the stores.

Now my dear reader I shall attempt to describe how we worked locomotives over the branch to the County town, so settle back into your favourite chair, and if you try hard, you may hear in your mind the shrill cry of a steam whistle, the steady exhaust beat of an approaching locomotive, and smell the distinctive aroma of hot oil and steam.

The years roll back to the early 1960s when a brand new Hillman Imp car would cost £508.including tax, fill up your tank with petrol at 4 gallons for a £1, and buy a 3-bed semi detached house with garage priced at £2,750.

I am now a young fireman again, booking on at Yeovil Town shed to work, the 7.05am passenger train to Taunton.

This is how it used to be.

It is one of those sunny mornings when from early daybreak the warmth of the air and a sky tinged with blue gave a foretaste of a glorious summer day to come.

It is around 5.30 am and I am cycling to work along Newton Road just a short distance from my home, wearing my regulation blue overalls, black tee shirt and grease proof cap, not exactly wanting to be up and about at that hour, but it was part and parcel of the job, and in any case, it was early start – early finish.

There is not much road traffic about at that time in the morning apart from milk floats and a few other early workers, amongst them a sprinkling of other footplatemen heading towards the Town station.

I can hear the sounds of the locomotive shed and yard, long before I arrive to book on at 05.38 - steam escaping from safety valves, a shrill whistle and the sight of smoke rising in the still air plus the aroma of steam locomotives as I cycle across the railway bridge and turning right off the main road, freewheel down the slope to the rear of the locomotive shed and place my bicycle into the almost full cycle rack.

The three road locomotive shed stands on the left, as I walk past the engine cleaners cabin a place which holds many memories of my locomotive cleaning days it was also home to the coalmen who were responsible for replenishing by steam crane the tenders and bunkers of locomotives.

The shed is bustling as engines are either in the process of preparation with drivers oiling up the rods and motions or being disposed with fireman shovelling out smokebox and char and cleaning out glowing clinker from fireboxes.

The aroma of hot oil, steam and smoke hangs heavily in the air. Heaps of smokebox ash, glowing clinker, discarded clinker shovels, ashpan rakes, old headlamps, lumps of coal strewn everywhere, and puddles of oily water were all part and parcel of a working locomotive shed.

The shed office was in an old detached building standing at the far end of the shed roads alongside the 'table' road. Entering the building and climbing the stairs, at the top was a room whereupon the booking on clerks were busy working at their desks, in front of which were an imposing bank of telephones, most of which were ringing continuously.

After booking on, it was time to descend the stairs to the locker room to collect my wooden enginemans box and tea can from my locker, into which I put my sandwiches (made by mother of course) plus a Lyons individual fruit pie (apple was my favourite) plus tea, sugar and milk to keep my driver and I going for the day, the box also contained soap and towel and various other odds and ends.

Another room at the bottom of the stairs was lined with glass cases containing all of the diagrams, working timetables and special notices affecting all of the duties involving Yeovil crews.

Time to meet my driver in the enginemens cabin which was situated next to the shed office, this would usually have at least a couple of crews or maybe more depending on the time of day sitting inside, furniture was basic but functional a couple of long tables plus long wooden forms, plus a gas ring and stone sink.

Enginemens cabins in all locomotive sheds were a debating chamber on all manner of subjects and various arguments could arise all of which I must state were without malice, although if certain people were known to 'bite' then the perpetrators would sail into them without mercy, the hapless victims would never learn!

Some of my best days in the railway service involved sitting in the enginemens cabin at Yeovil or at other steam sheds including Salisbury or Exmouth Junction nattering and arguing with my mates, there was, of course, a pecking order, with the senior drivers at the top of the tree, going down through the ranks to the passed firemen, firemen and passed cleaners.

The ever boiling kettle was always on the go day and night as crews booked on or off, and there was a daily stream of visiting crews from other sheds including Salisbury and Exmouth Junction who would have their tea and sandwiches between duties. But whatever the seniority of the person, we were all linked as footplatemen to a man – and Southern men at that. I took the chance to make a can of tea, to enjoy at Pen Mill.

Our shed had a good atmosphere, we had our own football team 'Railway United' and a skittle team which played at the Alexandra (known as the Alex) Hotel outside the front of the station.

Most of us were in the union ASLEF although a few were in the NUR and it must be said that if any man was in trouble of some kind, either workwise or personal, then we would pull together to help our comrade. It was more of a parochial atmosphere and probably would not happen in the 21st Century.

The Yeovil area employed a large number of railway staff in 1963, our shed alone had 120 footplate staff, twenty of whom were under 18 working as engine cleaners, Yeovil Pen Mill station had a staff of 30, Yeovil Town approx. 35, Yeovil Junction 40 plus 60 men at the track pre-assembly depot. The staff association social club at Pen Mill had over 300 branch members.

The future Beeching cuts, plus dieselisation and the Western Region take-over of the Southern Region lines west of Salisbury would have a devastating effect on staffing levels in the area.

The branch services between Taunton and Yeovil were worked under the following locomotive diagrams - Yeovil Duties No's 518, 520 521 and Taunton Duties 31 & 33; the Taunton-Yeovil freight (6.20am ex Taunton) came under Plymouth Duty 834 (Taunton footplatemen). When the Class 22 diesels were put to use on the branch in 1964 they were worked by Taunton men under Newton Abbot Duty No. 46.

It is now time for my driver and I to leave the clamour of the driver's cabin with its cigarette and pipe smoke filled atmosphere and find our locomotive.

We walk past a hissing S15 4-6-0 which is taking water from the column on No 1 shed road before reversing down for coaling and fire cleaning, a bit of banter with the crew who are also Yeovil men takes place between them and my mate and I.

The S15's known as 'blackuns' were superb mixed traffic engines and just the type of locomotive to have whilst working on heavy freight trains between Salisbury and Exeter on the severe banks such as Honiton, Chard and the climb from Gillingham to Semley, not once during my firing days did one of these engines let me down for steam.

Our locomotive is standing on the No2 shed road with a whisper of steam issuing from the safety valves, green paintwork shining in the summer sunshine she is No.5548 one of the ex GWR 4575 class 2-6-2 prairie tanks designed by George Jackson Churchward and built at Swindon in 1928 weighing 60 tons and fitted with the larger sloping water tanks holding 1,300 gallons, a coal bunker with a capacity of just over three tons. Classified as Group Yellow route availability, Power class C under the GWR system and Class 4MT in the B.R. Power class system.

No. 5548 was first allocated to Tyseley when built, and after spending time at Bristol Bath Road and Pen Mill sheds, ended her days at Yeovil Town and was withdrawn in June 1963.

This type of locomotive is capable of a top speed of 60mph if conditions were suitable, with leading and trailing wheels of 3' 2" and coupled wheels of 4' 7½" diameter plus a boiler pressure of 200 lb per sq. in. and a tractive effort of 21,250 lb.

The locomotive has already been prepared for us as we climb up into the warm cab and put our boxes and tea can away into the lockers provided, a good fire is burning away in the firebox with a good head of steam building up in the pressure gauge, time to turn on the steam blower valve a fraction to stop flames and fumes drifting into the cab from the firebox.

The boiler water gauge shows about a half a glass of water bobbing up and down in the glass tube, this reflects the state of water in the boiler, half a glass equates to the boiler being half full, more than enough to take us to Pen Mill.

Other checks take place, detonators and red flags for emergencies are in place in the locker, fire irons are in place on the water tanks, firing shovel, bucket are all there, water levels are checked in the tanks, the lubricator is turned on with a piece of paper inserted behind the sight feeds to check that the drops of oil are dropping through correctly.

After trimming any large lumps of coal in the bunker which might block the coalplate I turn on the injector and use the pep pipe to give the coal in the bunker a good soaking as we shall be running bunker first to Pen Mill, my mate has also been busy checking the oil trimmings etc.

The steam brake is applied by my driver in order that I can unwind the hand brake, the large vacuum ejector is released and the twin needles in the vacuum gauge climb to the regulation 25 inches, and my mate uses the last few minutes to start writing out the drivers ticket, this will be handed back into the shed office upon our return, this gives details of crew, engine number, timings and any occurrences etc. Head and tail lamps are in place and we are ready to go. Just time to light a woodbine for the run to Pen Mill.

A quick glance over each side to check that no other locomotives are moving in our vicinity, my mate asks me if I am ready, as he places the reverser into full forward gear, releases the steam brake and pulls the whistle cord giving a sharp blast on the whistle.

With steam roaring from our cylinders through the open cylinder cocks, our engine moves forward with a sudden beat from the chimney, time for me to close the firedoors to stop cold air being sucked into the firebox and onto the tubeplate.

My mate closes the cylinder cocks, as we pass the footplatemens cabin and shed office, ahead of us the shed starting signal is in the off position and just before this there are two ramps between the tracks, one is for the BR Automatic Warning System and the other is the ex GWR Automatic Train Control and as we pass over the GWR version the siren sounds in the cab, and my mate cancels the siren by lifting the lever on the system on his side of the cab.

The two ramps would give an audible caution warning to all locomotives leaving the depot. The difference with the BR system is that a visual warning as well as a sound warning is given, the shade on the box inside the cab would go to yellow accompanied by a warning siren when approaching a distant signal at caution, or with a distant signal in the clear position the shade would go black accompanied by the sound of the bell.

The ex GWR system comprised of a 44ft long steel ramp fixed between the rails on the approach to distant signals, a wire connected the ramp with a switch in the signalbox via a contact in the signal arm.

When the signalman operated the signal lever in the signalbox to place the distant signal in the clear position, the ramp was made live by an electric battery, a steel contact shoe fitted underneath the centre line of GWR locomotives made contact with the electrified ramp, making a bell ring in the locomotive cab.

With the signal arm at caution, or in the event of a battery failure, the ramp was 'dead' and when passing over the ramp, a siren would sound in the cab and the brakes would be automatically applied.

The driver on hearing the siren would operate the resetting handle on the ATC box in the cab, thereby stopping the siren and overriding the automatic brake application.

As we run past the shed starting signal at our booked departure time of 05.53 the signalman in the Town box is busy with his signal levers as the signal slams to danger behind us and the protecting catch points open.

We proceed under Stars lane footbridge and come to a halt just beyond the ground signals, the water bobs up and down in the gauge glass, and I open the dampers to bring air up through the firebars, the steady thump of the fire burning through as steam pressure is climbing towards the red mark, due to the fire being uplifted with our exhaust beat on the short journey from the shed, smoke mixes with steam from the chimney in the early sunshine.

My mate puts the lever into reverse gear, and now its time to run bunker first as the points switch and the ground signal clangs over, the locomotive now runs over the crossover points guiding us onto the GWR branch line and towards the signal box, the heat is building up on the footplate as I cross over to the drivers side of the cab, just as we glide to a halt outside the signal box, the window opens and the signalman hands me the large hoop holding the single line tablet for Pen Mill.

I can hear the sound of block bells and instruments ringing through the open window; this is a busy signal box, containing a 55 lever frame controlling not only the line from here to Hendford and Pen Mill but also train services and light engine movements to and from Yeovil Junction, plus shunting in the station area and locomotives entering and leaving the shed.

The ex GWR single line was always known as the main, and the double track route to Yeovil Junction as the branch. The box was open continuously.

After checking that the correct single line tablet Yeovil Town-Yeovil Pen Mill is in the hoop; I hang it up in the corner of the cab as we pick up speed and rattle along the platform through the Town station, the gentle beat of our exhaust echoes around the station as ahead of us the platform starter for the line to Pen Mill is already lowered, this signal also shares the same post as the Pen Mill up branch fixed distant signal, as with a blast on the whistle warning of our approach to any member of the station staff using the barrow crossing we run under the footbridge and Newton road bridge heading for our destination.

It only takes a few minutes before we coast to a halt at the Pen Mill up branch outer home which is at danger, time for me to climb down open the box at the bottom of the signal post and use the telephone to report to the signalman, the conversation would usually go like this 'light engine, complete with tail lamp for the 7.05 Taunton stopped at up branch outer home' the signalman would usually reply, that we would be stopped for a few minutes etc, and the signal arm would eventually lower with a metallic clang.

With the road clear we would start off again and round the corner near the abandoned Pen Mill locomotive shed, and past the inner home signal which is clear and rumble over the points connecting us with the Weymouth main line curving in from our right.

We pass under the A30 Sherborne road overbridge and my mate closes the regulator as we coast into the station and stop at the signalbox situated at the London end of the down platform, here the signalman collects the single line token from us. The box at Pen Mill containing a 65-lever frame dates from 1937, controlling not only the section to Marston Magna but also the section to Yeovil South Junction and Yetminster plus the branch to Yeovil Town.

There was no need to give up the single line token at the signalbox, as a small secondary token instrument was housed in a small hut at the Weymouth end of the down platform, working in conjunction with the signalbox, this was very useful, especially if one of the platform staff collected the single line token from an incoming branch train, and placed it through the platform instrument to clear the branch line, especially when a fresh engine was already waiting to take the train back to Taunton.

We are booked to freight shunting duties between 6.00 and 6.45 am in the down goods yard which was a busy place to work, handling large amounts of freight to and from the main shunting yard at Hendford, and transfer traffic to Yeovil Junction and Templecombe, all of which went via Yeovil Town.

Two freight trains amongst others, namely the Severn Tunnel and East Depot services from Bristol would bring a vast amount of wagons to be shunted off for the Yeovil area.

After a bout of shunting in the down yard we were booked to shunt our own coaches between 6.45 & 6.55 this would be formed of four carriages, usually 2 'B' Sets which would usually be found in the up sidings near the goods shed. Other carriages including four coach 'M' sets would also be used on the branch services.

YEOVIL PEN MILL LOCOMOTIVE SHED

Originally constructed to house broad-gauge locomotives, the shed occupied a site in the vee of land created by the main line to Weymouth and the branch to Yeovil Town.

At first built as a two road shed of wooden construction measuring 102ft x 40ft, an additional single road extension built on to the side of the main building near the Yeovil Town branch and measuring 102ft x 20ft was completed in 1877. In later years this was used as a repair shop.

A 33,000 gallon water tank formed the roof of the 30ft x 20ft coaling platform, whilst a small 44ft 8in turntable was situated at the rear of the shed near the Town branch.

This turntable was equipped in 1928 with extension bars, known to enginemen as 'skis' a small mogul or 22xx 0-6-0 could be turned with difficulty, and known to many visiting enginemen as 'that pig of a table'.

Two breakdown tool vans and a snowplough were allocated to the depot.

The late Fred Martin with whom I shared many a footplate, in weather fair or foul, good trip or bad, was a superb driver to work with, not only for his skill in handling locomotives, but also for the man himself, always good humoured, always with a cheery whistle, even when things may be going wrong (as happened at times) on the footplate. I feel privileged to have known and worked with him.

Fred had started as an engine cleaner at Yeovil Pen Mill locomotive shed in 1937 and had been one of the ex GWR drivers moved to our shed at Yeovil Town in 1959 when Pen Mill shed closed. He was very popular, as a tribute to his memory I now include the following memory of Pen Mill shed as written by him for me some years ago.

'My cleaning days, well there is not much to tell really, there were six cleaners, 2 on each shift 6am-2pm, 2pm-10.pm, 10pm-6am, all the engines were oiled down and cleaned to perfection, you had to be 18 years old to go on night work.

When I started I was about 17 so I was on day turn for a 12 month. When I did start nights, one cleaner went on duty at midnight Sunday night in order to do what they term as call-boy all the week. He called out men on early turns to make sure they got to work, that was from 2.15am – 6.00am.

When you had 52 spare firing turns in as a cleaner, you were rewarded with an overcoat, and if you called the breakdown gang out, after riding all around the town to find them, we went with them in the breakdown vans and were paid an extra shilling.

The loco shed at Pen Mill consisted of 10 engines and two spare ones, which were all used on double or treble shifts one way or the other, banking turns, goods trains, and branch passenger trains. Pannier tanks for shunting, side tanks 55-class etc for branch passenger work.

As we all know, the branch line Yeovil P.M. to Langport is a single track and is worked on a staff system, some people call it a staff which has a key on one end for unlocking ground frames, and some call it tablet or token, but the real name is the 'staff of life' it was given to the signalman at every station by the fireman, and in return he would exchange it for another one, in order to pass you through the next section, which you did on the Yeovil to Taunton branch.

The first freight train out in the morning was the Hendford Goods about 5.30am, which cleared the traffic from the night before for all merchants in and around the Yeovil area. Messrs Bradfords, Burts, Coop coal and timber, Esso petrol with their storage tank at the far end of Hendford goods yard for Westland Aircraft, which it was called then. The engine stopped at Hendford shunting until dinner time, when it returned to Pen Mill for relief and back again.

In the meantime another goods left Yeovil P.M. at 10.00am which was termed as the Langport goods, this had anything up to 25-35 wagons on for putting off en-route, this train was mainly for Martock which also had coal for the gas works, coal for Bradfords, cow cake for farmers, coal for private traders, building materials-bricks, cement, all of this had to be shunted out and put into place, it was all what you would call – happy days, one big family together.

On leaving Martock we run to Langport and put the rest of our train away, which is about the same comprising, coal, cow cake, bricks etc, we stay shunting until 3.15pm, pick up the traffic we have shunted and run back to Thorney Halt, collect the loaded milk vans, then back to Martock, put the milk vans into the siding which also held a loaded meat van. A light engine would arrive from Pen Mill to collect the milk and meat vans and run back to Yeovil Town. This engine would also be booked to work a transfer goods train to Yeovil Junction from Pen Mill via the Town station.

There was nothing to get excited about, because you were too busy, until they started to run it down, everybody had their job to do, and it was a very busy branch.

During the war years, we had troop, ambulance, tank and ammunition trains, the ambulance trains went to the U.S.Army hospital at Norton Fitzwarren.

An instance occurred during the war, when our Spitfire pilots used to practice strafing trains, very often you were looking over the side or looking forward, you would see two streaks and a spinner coming towards you, which put a nasty taste in my mouth for a moment, but glad to say, a main line driver stopped at Curry Rivel Junction signal box a few weeks later, and the practice soon stopped.

The Southern Railway had a turn, when a light engine came over from Yeovil Town and transferred goods to Yeovil Junction and return to Pen Mill, the train was shunted out and taken to Westbury, and we also had coal trains for Yeovil Town and Exmouth Junction.

Pen Mill shed had only four or five turns working passenger trains on the branch, and Taunton men had about the same, the 7.05am from Yeovil stopped at Yeovil Town and all stations to Taunton, we would return to Yeovil with the 9.45am and upon arrival at Pen Mill would proceed with shunting until relief arrived.

Another crew would book on at 9.45am, prepare engine and off shed at 10.30am come out on train, and change over with Taunton men on goods, work to Martock and Langport shunting, and carry on to Athelney, changeover with Taunton men working a passenger train, work back to Pen Mill and get relief.

A crew rostered to work at 2.15pm would go shunting, and then work the 5.50pm to Taunton returning with the 8.15pm to Yeovil.

As I was saying earlier, the Yeovil to Taunton branch was a very busy line, farmers from the villages for miles around, brought their sugar beet to the stations and loaded into wagons by the ton, meaning 6 to 8 wagons which used to carry 12 tons each when loaded.

They were picked up at each station, made up into a train and transported to Kidderminster and refined for sugar. The same thing with cattle, loaded into wagons at each station for the slaughterhouses, and used to work out 25-30 wagons when made up.

The small loco shed was not only for branch work as we had banking engines from Yeovil Pen Mill to Evershot, or assisting engines as some people called it.

Night banking engines at Castle Cary to Witham, goods trains to Westbury, and a goods train from Castle Cary to Durston, shunting everywhere down the main line en route.

Another service worked by Yeovil men was the 4.25 Taunton to Yeovil and upon arrival at Pen Mill, the train then formed the 5.56 to Trowbridge with a booked arrival of 7.14pm.

The little bit of branch work I have explained is a little of what used to go on, we also used to grumble about the turns of duty and one thing and another. But given the same chance, and the steam locomotive back. I would do the same again (although I did time on diesels). But steam was our life'.

I can honestly state that I can not remember one fireman at our shed that did not like working with Fred. The world is a poorer place without him.

YEOVIL DUTY No. 518.
4 M.T. (45 XX Class)

—	Yeovil Loco.	5.53 a.m.	‖
5.58 a.m.	Yeovil P.M....	—	
	F—Shunting 6.0 a.m. to 6.45 a.m.		
	C—Shunting 6.45 a.m. to 6.55 a.m.		
—	Yeovil P.M....	7. 5 a.m.	P
8.17 a.m.	Taunton	9.45 a.m.	P
10.45 a.m.	Yeovil Pen Mill ...	11.21 a.m.	P
12.21 p.m.	Taunton	**	‖
**	Loco. Yard...	4. 5 p.m.	P
**	Taunton	4.25 p.m.	P
5.37 p.m.	Yeovil P.M....	5.54 p.m.	‖
5.59 p.m.	Yeovil Loco.	9. 0 p.m.	‖
9. 5 p.m.	Pen Mill	—	
	F—Shunting 9.30 p.m. to 10.50 p.m.		
—	Yeovil Pen Mill ...	10.50 p.m.	‖
10.55 p.m.	Yeovil T.	11. 3 p.m.	F
	(10.40 p.m. Yeovil Jc.)		
11. 5 p.m.	Pen Mill	—	
	F—Shunting 11.20 p.m. to 12.0 mdt.		
—	Pen Mill	12.10 a.m.	‖
12.15 a.m.	Yeovil T.	12.30 a.m.	F
	(12.1 a.m. Yeovil Jc.)		
12.35 a.m.	Pen Mill	12.50 a.m.	F
		A.R. (Q)	
1.22 a.m.	Maiden Newton ...	1.45 a.m.	‖
2.17 a.m.	Yeovil Loco.	—	

Nos. 4593 & 9663 prepare to leave Yeovil Pen Mill station for Taunton with the Quantock Flyer Rail Tour on 16 February 1964.

Authors Collection

YEOVIL PEN MILL TO HENDFORD

We are now standing at the Weymouth end of the up platform coupled onto our coaches. The 'up' is a reversible platform, meaning that trains can be signalled to leave from either direction, the starting signal had a destination box which would show: - Engine shed, Down Branch, Up Branch, Down main.

The time is ticking away to our departure time of 7.05am, last minute things to do include placing the headlamp from the buffer beam to its place on the top bracket on the smokebox and take our lamp off the rear buffer beam.

Back on the footplate the fire is throbbing away, the steam pressure is near the red mark, and the water is bobbing up and down in the gauge glass, the dampers are open and the aroma of hot oil and steam drifts around the platform, the locomotive is alive and ready for the off, our exhaust is crackling as the vacuum gauge needles quiver at their maximum of 25inches.

The fire is swelling rapidly and time to put the injector on as the safety valves start to lift, a quick swill around the cab floor with the pep pipe to keep the dust down, and then turn off the steam and water valves as there is enough water in the boiler for the moment. The footplate on this class of locomotive was cramped, as the side water tanks were set back into the cab, with the fireman standing in a well in the floor when firing. And to swing one of the fire irons, such as a pricker or dart around the cab, was not the easiest thing to accomplish.

I have caught the end of a fire iron, such as a clinker shovel, on the whistle chain, more than once whilst trying to get it into the firebox, to stir the fire up, whilst scraping clinker from the firebars.

Seating being confined to a pair of pull down wooden flaps, it was not possible to sit down and watch the road ahead at the same time, so you had the choice of standing up and looking out through the cab windows along the top of the boiler with steam and smoke beating down from the chimney, or looking out over the side of the cab, and on a hot summer day, the latter choice would suit me.

Just enough tea left for my mate and I as our two mugs are filled from my billy can which has been kept warm on the shelf above the firedoor. And like all firemen it was wise to know each driver's preferences with regards to a cup of tea. Some liked it strong, some weak, plenty of sugar or none at all, some liked cold tea, but I have never met a driver who didn't like tea.

Whilst we are knocking back our tea, the guard comes up, gives us the load, takes the drivers name and locomotive number for his journal, and after a bit of banter, he strolls back along the platform to the rear of the train.

I look back along the platform from the drivers side of the cab, the platform staff are loading parcels etc into the guards van in the rear coach, passengers are walking along the platform to join our train, and the W.H.Smith bookstall is already open and selling newspapers and magazines.

We are the first passenger train to leave Pen Mill this morning, the down passenger train 5.45am from Bristol Temple Meads will not arrive until 07.39 and the first up 7.17am from Weymouth will not arrive until 8.23am.

An engine spotter on a summer Saturday during the 1950's at Yeovil Pen Mill would have a field day as a grand variety of ex GWR locomotives worked through on the main line to and from Weymouth.

Castle, County, Grange and Manor class locomotives would be seen, plus B.R. Standard class locomotives. Prairie and pannier tanks would be working local services and banking trains up the severe ascent between Yetminster and Evershot.

As well as the regular timetable services, there would be excursion trains as well as the Swindon Works holiday trains running to Weymouth.The star train of the day was the 'Channel Islands Boat Express' running from Paddington to Weymouth. Unfortunately this fine service was withdrawn from 2nd November 1959 with transfer to the Waterloo-Weymouth route.

Glancing back along the platform reminds me of trips to Bristol with my father and brother to visit my uncle and aunt in the late 1940s, this was (unknown to us boys at the time) during the last years of the GWR.

Standing on the crowded platform, a shout would resound around the platform from a member of the station staff '*Bristol Train' Bristol Train*' and a huge green painted, hissing, smoking leviathan with a bright orange glow from the firebox, would thunder into the station, making the platform tremble, before bringing the train of coaches to a halt with a squealing of brakes.

Enough of boyhood days, we have a train to work. Time to place a few shovelfulls of coal into the back corners of the firebox, not too much as the firebox is crammed full. This class of engine likes to have the back corners, and under the firedoor packed solid, and sloping down to the front end, unlike a pannier tank which likes a saucer shaped fire to make them steam well.

The heat is tremendous in the cab as the minute's tick away to our departure time; the safety valves start to lift as the shunter hands us the single line tablet – Yeovil Pen Mill – Yeovil Town in its steel hoop, the lower quadrant arm on the platform starter has already been lowered and showing 'Down Branch' in the destination box.

I have closed the firedoors as the sound of the guards whistle echoes along the platform at 7.05am precisely - time to go.

My mate opens the regulator, and we move forward with a sigh from the cylinders and a sharp exhaust blast from the chimney. The 45xx 2-6-2 prairie tank engines had a habit of going down on their springs and roll when pulling away from a stop.

A quick check back along the train on the drivers side, just in case any mad fool tries to board the train at the last minute, no such trouble this time as I cross back to my side of the footplate as we swing over onto the down main line passing under the A30 overbridge, before the points switch us over the up main line and onto the branch with the coach wheels squealing in protest as they follow us over the crossover.

We run past the old GWR shed again, as our engine gets into its stride and is notched up into mid gear with the regulator cracked half open as we pass the Pen Mill down branch advanced starter which has the distant signal permanently fixed at caution for Yeovil Town on the same post.

The whole engine is alive and quivering with power, the firedoors rattle as the exhaust beats down onto the fire, water bounces up and down in the gauge glass and steam beats down from our chimney and trails back down over our following coaches, the resounding beat of the exhaust and the slap of the vacuum pump resounds against the steep wooded side of Wyndham Hill to our right, whilst to our left the ground slopes down to the tree lined banks of the river Yeo.

There is no need to tend to the fire on this short stretch of our journey, as I open the firedoors and place the firing flap in place to keep the engine quiet as we approach Yeovil Town station. The regulator is closed and the reverser thrown into full forward gear, with a touch on the blower valve to stop the fire blowing back into the cab.

The double track branch to Yeovil Junction is on my side of the locomotive and with the down branch home signal lowered, and long blast on our whistle, my mate gives a slight brake application, there is a large hiss from the ejector, the needles in the vacuum gauge suddenly drop down from

25inches as the vacuum is destroyed, the smell of hot brake blocks biting against our driving wheels combined with the aroma of coal smoke and steam from our chimney wafts back into the cab.

We run under the road and footbridge making our noisy entrance into the station, passengers move forward on to the 450 yard long platform 1 to catch our train, porters with barrows loaded with parcels await near the platform edge to load the luggage van at the rear of the train.

We rumble past the buffet serving the first of many customers for the day, and with my mate making a final brake application, come to a stand with a squeal of brakes at the end of the platform spot on time at 07.07 we have three minutes allotted to us here, not a lot of time to spare as we have to cross the 06.45 from Taunton at Martock.

A glance across at the Platform 2 shows us the familiar shape of one of our Drummond M7 0-4-4 tanks with its Westinghouse air pump panting away (we had two at Yeovil 30129 and 30131) coupled on to its push and pull set, waiting to propel the 07.22 to Yeovil Junction, this is the first of many trips run between the Town and Junction stations until the last run at 9.52pm to Pen Mill and return.

The crews on the Town-Junction shuttles will be working on Yeovil Diagram 517, with the first set booking on at 6.50am and off shed with locomotive and push & pull set at 7.05, (the engine having been prepared by another crew) relieved by a second set of men at 2.40pm.

This would not have been the first passenger service working out of the Town station in the morning as the 6.25 to Ilfracombe and 6.55 to Salisbury have already departed.

However, back on our footplate I have turned off the injector, after squeezing more water into the boiler to keep the engine quiet, and using the pep pipe to swill down the cab floor, and damp down the coal in the bunker, we have more than enough steam for our purposes, my mate is happy and puffing on his cigarette, and our locomotive – she is quivering with energy and ready for the off.

WYNDHAM PALMER – SHUNTING TRACTOR, COWS, ELEPHANTS AND ERROL FLYNN

Wyndham Palmer after completing his National Service began work as a goods porter at Yeovil Town station in 1952.

'I used to cycle in from my home in Martock, or at times catch the early train. I used to drive the shunter tractor which was equipped with buffers front and rear, the goods yard was at right angles to the Town station, trucks were pushed through the goods shed by steam locomotives, then we would split them up one at a time by our tractor for the sidings in the goods yard.

There were three wagon turntables in the yard, and traffic consisted of coal, scrap metal, bananas, plus general traffic in goods vans. Our first job in the mornings was to unload the goods vans in the shed, then start up the tractor and proceed to Johnny Farr's siding shunting the trucks which were full of scrap metal, then shunt coal trucks into the traders sidings and also coal into the gas works. We used to wander into the gas works, which was an interesting place to visit, as the large coal trucks were tipped into hoppers, the coal being fed into furnaces.

A chap called Macveigh worked with me in the yard, and we used to 'fly shunt' wagons with our tractor, I used the tractor to push the wagon on, and my mate was ready by the point lever, the wagon would hit the buffer block and bounce back into the siding, one day whilst shunting we went too far, and the wagon instead of hitting the buffer block and bouncing back, went straight through and nearly ended up in Middle Street!

Friday being market day, the cows would be herded down from the market to the station, we used to use between 30 and 40 cattle wagons in the back road near the goods shed, at the cattle pens we would load 5 or 6 trucks at a time, the pilot loco would take them away, and replace them with another 5 or 6, we also used to load calves, but they went by horse boxes.

We had one cow on a particular day, which was put into the cattle pens, awaiting for a truck, and be taken away, we went off into the goods shed to work, then after about two hours, someone said, the cow has got out, we looked, and sure enough the cow had gone.

Apparently I found out afterwards, that the smell of animal bones in a nearby truck awaiting despatch to a glue factory, had upset the animal. The cow meanwhile had wandered up to the nearby Aplin & Barretts factory and was trampling over the workers bicycles.

Me and Macveigh went up to the factory and managed to pen the animal between the buildings and put a rope on his horns, then myself, Mac and a bloke we used to call Errol Flynn, so named because he looked like the film star, and also had a quiff, led the cow back to the station, with myself holding on to the animal's nose, Mac on the rope, and Errol Flynn had the cows tail twisted, just as we got back to the station gate, the animal smelt the bones again, and flicked and twisted and got away again, the market then had to send someone down to shoot the animal.

Bertram Mills Circus used to visit and unload in the yard, we would see the elephants come in, and I would be walking through the yard by the goods vans, and you feel something in your pocket, this would be an elephants trunk. That was good fun.

Whilst pushing a load of empty coal wagons through the goods shed one day to connect with the train to take them away, the shunter was waving me on, when all of a sudden the trucks moved fast, and I reversed my tractor off the line, the head shunter appeared shouting 'we are off the road', unfortunately when I was propelling the wagons out of the shed, Tom Best the station shunter, at the same time was pulling cattle wagons out of the pens, all of the wagons met at the end of the goods shed, which resulted in a bogie siphon 'G' being tipped over on to its side with empty milk churns inside, I had one hours overtime to unload the empty churns.

Banana vans used to arrive five or six at a time and had to be unloaded in the goods shed, I used to be wary of the hairy spiders concealed in the hand's of bananas, all of this traffic was collected by lorry from local produce merchants, Banbury's of Earle Street and Drakes in Huish.

I had an interesting job with good mates and worked in the goods yard for 5 years before moving to Thorney Halt.

Thankyou Wyndham we will meet you at Montacute.

Ahead of us on my side of the cab, the upper quadrant platform starter is raised, and beyond that the intermediate starting signal is also clear, at our departure time of 7.10 the sound of the guards whistle, plus the waving of his green flag gives us the 'right away'.

With a sharp bark from our chimney so typical of ex GWR locomotives we pull away from the platform, time to look back along the train from the driver's side, after checking that everything behind us is ok. Now is the time to prepare for the token exchange.

The signal box at Yeovil Town was located at the Hendford end of the W.R. branch platform, so it was time to cross back again to my mate's side of the cab and exchange the hoop from the Pen Mill section for the long brass baton which is inscribed Yeovil Town – Hendford, an awkward item compared to a hoop, so place it in the bucket out of the way.

Back over on my side of the cab, a glance towards the locomotive shed shows the familiar scene of smoke and steam drifting around the locomotive yard. No time to stand looking about, we have a train to work, run on time and get our passengers to their destination in safety.

The reverser is eased back and the regulator cracked open wider as we pass under the footbridge that spans all tracks at this end of the Town station connecting Stars Lane with Summerhouse Hill a favourite location for engine spotters, and the place where most photographs of the station and locomotive shed have been taken over many years.

Glove factories and tanneries stand alongside the track on our right, factories that once made Yeovil a household name for some of the best gloves in Great Britain are sadly just a memory now.

I place a few rounds of coal into the firebox just under the door, close the bunker flap to stop coal dust from flying around the cab as we pass the advanced starting signal with its upper quadrant arm raised to the sky ushering us onwards to Hendford, we roll under the road bridge and around the curve in the track, another set of rails runs parallel to us, this is the long siding which stretches all the way from the Town station to Hendford Halt.

This is the original Salisbury & Yeovil line operated by the L&SWR when opened to Hendford in 1860 sharing station facilities with the Bristol & Exeter Railway until Yeovil Town station opened in 1861, and used as a siding, in my firing days for storing coaching stock, known to all Yeovil staff as 'up over heaven'.

My mate is looking at the road ahead through the cab window and his hand is not far away from the brake handle, just in case of an emergency as we pound towards Hendford with our locomotive swaying and pounding to the sound of our exhaust beat and the lovely slap of the vacuum pump at work.

Time for me to take a quick lean over the side of the cab and get a breath of fresh air in the summer sunshine, but not for long, as coal dust soon starts swirling around, time to turn the water and steam valves on for the injector to pump more water into the boiler, and use the pep pipe to spray water around the cab floor and into the bunker in order to keep the coal dust down.

No.4593 has been shunting in Hendfords Goods all day, and now waits alongside Hendford Halt signal box before leaving with the 6.10pm transfer freight to Yeovil Junction. *John Day*

HENDFORD TO MARTOCK

HENDFORD HALT & HENDFORD GOODS

The wooded area leading to the beauty spot of nine springs can be seen to our left as the fixed distant signal for Hendford appears ahead.

A public footpath crosses the branch line and siding here, controlled by a whistle board, a blast on our whistle heralds our approach, whilst my mate closes the regulator, placing the reverser into full forward gear and giving the steam blower a turn to stop the fire blowing back into the cab

Smoke and steam billow from our chimney, the sound of our exhaust echoes under the Hendford Hill roadbridge as we pass through the brick lined cutting, ahead of us is a two arm gantry with the right hand signal arm lowered guiding us towards the platform.

We rattle over the points leading into Hendford Goods yard to our right, this is known as 'Hendford Goods Junction' the yard is packed full of freight wagons, there is no sign of the shunting engine, or indeed of the shunters, they are probably having a fry up in the cabin at the far end of the yard.

The vacuum brake is being applied, and again the smell of hot brake blocks biting into our driving wheels drifts into the cab, our coaches start to drag as the blocks start to bite against the bogie wheels and our locomotive speed starts to decrease.

The small signal box stands to our left, and ahead of us standing alongside the track, is the figure of the signalman with the brass baton for the section ahead to Martock in his upraised hand.

Time to make another exchange as I pick up the baton from the Town station and lean out of the cab in readiness, the prairie tank engines being higher than pannier tanks meant that the fireman had to lean down to effect the exchange with the signalman standing on the ground, and although we would be slowing down, with my mate working the vacuum brake into the engine, we would still be running in at a fair speed.

This meant that there would be no room for error, and I have often seen some worried looks from signalmen standing alongside the track, as a wack on the head would be no joke, and I knew of a signalman who was knocked unconscious by an incorrect changeover.

However no problems as the exchange is accomplished safely, and we receive the Hendford-Martock single line staff, which is placed in the bucket out of the way as our locomotive and coaches squeal to a halt at the end of the single platform halt which is on the drivers side of the cab, we both look back along the platform to view what passengers we have either joining or leaving the train with a slamming of coach doors.

The halt platform was sparsely furnished with a wooden shelter and gas lighting and used mainly by workers from the adjacent Westland Helicopter factory, even more so during the severe winter of 1962/63 with most of the West of England covered by snow and ice, when the only transport available to most people was via the good old reliable train.

Hendford Goods was the busiest shunting yard in Yeovil with its various sidings serving the local traders plus a 150ft goods shed at the far end of the yard adjacent to the Horsey Lane entrance, the goods shed contained three 30cwt cranes, and would contain approximately seven wagons, whilst out in the yard area there were two yard cranes of 30cwt and 10 tons capacity, plus cattle pens, a carriage landing, the whole yard could contain a total of 139 wagons. Yeovil Town Loco had supplied the shunting locomotive since 1959 and for aeons previously by Pen Mill loco shed until its closure.

As a young fireman I always found the shunting duty at Hendford rather tedious, up and down the sidings banging and thumping the wagons about, it wasn't a hard turn to work, and as long as the fire was kept up under the firedoor, with enough steam without raising the safety valves, that's all you wanted. But I was always pleased to return to firing duties on the main line between Salisbury and Exeter.

I remember the regular drivers on the yard shunter very well. Joe Swaffield had started on the GWR before the Second World War and had worked all over the system in his footplate days, he had a fastidious habit of cleaning the backhead of the boiler at every opportunity, even to the extent of polishing behind the copper pipes with a stick and oily rag. The boiler front would shine like a new pin, and suffice to say, any fireman booked with Joe would also be indoctrinated into the extra special cleaning required.

The first goods 5.10am ex Pen Mill was usually a very heavy train, comprising of some forty or more wagons at times, many of the wagons were left on the main line (the branch was always known as the 'main' line, upon arrival, until the yard was sorted out, this was ok as the first passenger train from Pen Mill wasn't due until 7.15am, the excess traffic was then placed on the long siding.

The first job for the early turn pilot engine was to place the box vans into the goods shed, then the various traders sidings were sorted out, including coal, cement, bricks and basic slag for Messrs Bradford's, timber and coal for Burts, coal for the Co-op, petrol & diesel for Esso, animal feeds for Silcock's and Bibby's plus traffic for the Castrol oil store, and Lyons tea store.

A transfer freight conveying box vans from Nine Elms for the goods shed, petrol from Fawley, and cement for onwards shipment to Bridgwater via Durston would arrive from Yeovil Junction at approx. 7.15am, the locomotive which would range from a 'King Arthur' to a Class 4 Standard would leave the train at the top of the goods yard, returning light engine to Yeovil Town shed.

Shunting would cease around 7.45 am, the aroma of frying would waft from the door, the cabin known to all as 'the black hole' was situated at the end of the yard near the goods shed, and I in turn with many of my footplate comrades from the Town locomotive shed over the years, have enjoyed many a breakfast, and a good yarn in the cabin with shunters Eric Reeves and Mike Herrin.

After our short break, around 8.30am or so, it was back onto the locomotive to resume shunting, the shunters would also climb aboard, and we would set sail towards the top end of the yard, where the 6.20am daily pick-up goods from Taunton had left a couple of wagons, before continuing onwards to Pen Mill station, the goods train crewed by Taunton men would return at 10.30am dropping off more wagons.

Once a week, the Taunton goods dropped off, amongst other wagons, a box van containing bottles of spirits for the local brewery Messrs Bruttons. This load was valued at £600, which was quite an amount in the 1960's. Another Southern transfer freight would arrive about 11.00am and would be shunted into the yard dropping off its wagons, also collecting traffic to return to the Town station at 11.30am.

The goods shed was quite busy, with the first wagons in the morning shunted in from the early goods from Pen Mill, and when empty would be moved out, and replaced with traffic from the 7.15 transfer, and shunted again with wagons off the 11.00am transfer. Lorries and vans would be busy delivering goods from the shed to all parts of Yeovil and surrounding countryside.

The sidings were continuously being shunted to keep the traders supplied, the empties including petrol tankers and empty vans for return to the Southern Region being moved into the long siding up past the signal box in preparation for the 18.10 transfer freight to Yeovil Junction.

Wagons were also being marshalled for the 20.22 freight to Westbury throughout the day, and all day long the clank of buffers would be heard around the yard, as the shunting engine plodded up and down the various sidings.

The early turn footplate crew would leave Hendford at about 12.00pm returning light engine to Yeovil Town shed, fill up the tanks with water, and leave a large fire burning under the door and book off.

At 12.30pm the late turn crew would book on and depart light engine to Hendford, where between 1 & 2pm when their employees would be at lunch, empty wagons in the sidings of Messrs Bradford's, Burt's, the Co-op and Esso would be shunted out and replaced with full wagons taken from the long siding, then it would be time to travel along to Westland's siding before returning and resuming shunting duties in the goods yard.

The late turn pilot engine after shunting was completed, would then stand on the long siding alongside the signal box, where the fireman would build up the fire, his driver would take the chance to do a spot of oiling, and after the 17.45 Yeovil - Taunton passenger had cleared the section, would then work the 18.10 transfer freight from Hendford to Yeovil Junction and after putting the train away in the up sidings for remarshalling would return light engine to Yeovil Town to leave the locomotive on the disposal pits, the crew would catch the branch train to Yeovil Junction and relieve Salisbury men arriving with the 18.10 Salisbury - Yeovil Town, usually worked by a S15 4-6-0 although at times I have known a Bulleid Pacific allocated to this duty.

After uncoupling running around and re-attaching, the coaches would be hauled to Yeovil Town, the locomotive would run around and propel the coaches up as far as 'Nine Springs' where most of the empty coaching stock working out of Yeovil Town was stored, this location known to generations of Yeovil railwaymen as 'up over heaven'.

After uncoupling, and waiting for the shunter to climb aboard, the crew would return to Yeovil Town shed, leave the locomotive on the disposal pit at the bottom of the coal road, get their kit together, walk up to the shed office and book off, before entering the drivers cabin, for a wash and a bit of banter with other crews before going home for supper

We are standing at the end of the small platform at Hendford Halt, with our locomotive on the boil, quivering and ready to go, the heat from our roaring fire reflects against the rear of the cab, the injector is singing away until I turn off the steam and water valves, the reverser is in full forward gear, the vacuum gauge needles are quivering away and the last of our passengers are climbing aboard the coaches with a slamming of doors.

While we await the guards whistle, my good friend Mike Herrin describes his shunting days at Hendford.

MEMORIES OF SHUNTING DAYS AT HENDFORD GOODS RECALLED BY MIKE HERRIN

'Drive along Lysander Road in Yeovil today in the 21st Century and there is little evidence to suggest that this was once a busy railway yard, what were once green fields through which the branch line wove its way alongside the bulk of Westlands Aircraft factory has now given way to dense housing, and the busy Lysander road link, but to generations of Yeovil railwaymen, instead of the present occupiers such as PC World, Morrisons and MacDonalds they would be more at home with the Crane Road, Deal or Burts siding to name but a few of the 'roads' in Hendford yard.

The footpath at the rear of the present day PC World store leading to the leisure centre through the high sided brick built cutting was once the trackbed of the Bristol & Exeter Railway the first railway to serve Yeovil. And one set of rails, known as the Long Siding where loaded wagons were stored waiting their turn to be unloaded in the various traders sidings.

I started working at Hendford yard as a Shunter in late 1959 soon after becoming 18 years of age, a shunting pilot locomotive was employed in the yard for 11½ hours a day on an early and late shift, crewed mainly by two 'green card' men, namely Joe Swaffield and Bob Parker (alas now both deceased) as drivers, paired very often with a young passed engine cleaner as fireman, the pilot engine was a good way to introduce cleaners to the art of firing a locomotive.

We worked as a team, two shunters on the ground, and the loco crew, shunting was a hard job, but we had some fun, you walked or ran miles in a shift, wet through several times a day in the winter and soaked in sweat through the summer months, the job was not really heavy, although the skill required to flick the couplings over the drawhooks with the six foot shunting pole took a bit of mastering.

I worked with fellow shunter Eric Reeves for most of my time at Hendford; he was a really grand mate. I still see him around Yeovil and believe I owe my outlook on life to Eric, he has a unique way with him, and is a real gentleman.

Instead of describing a normal day in the yard, in and out of the sidings, with nothing out of the ordinary happening. I will recall some of the incidents and derailments etc that were a regular part of a busy shunting yard, but don't get the idea that it was a dangerous or unsafe place to work.

I guess the Health and Safety man would not be too happy today, for in my shunting days you could 'come off the road' or 'down on old England' (derailment) and if the running line was not involved thereby not hampering services on the branch line, or by not calling out the 'vans' (referring to the breakdown vans kept at Yeovil Town shed) you stood a fair chance of the incident escaping the attention of management.

A quick telephone call to Tom Setter the Carriage and Wagon man at Yeovil Pen Mill would bring him and his wheel gauge over on the next train. The offending wagon would be re-railed with some timber packing and a chain, or a lorry jack obtained from the nearby road motor department plus a couple of greased iron plates, 'back on the way she went off' was the norm.

The wagon was placed in a siding for Tom to check over, if any slight damage had occurred, a 'green card' trip to Pen Mill for attention was called for, and everything was squared up.

Unfortunately my first derailment at Hendford did involve calling out the 'vans' and was one incident that Tom could not deal with quietly.

We had virtually finished work for the day. Eric had gone home, and because of a vacancy we were working 12-hour shifts. I had the locomotive a 45xx 2-6-2 tank in the middle of a raft of wagons, propelling the wagons on the rear of the loco out towards the long siding to attach to and form the 6.10pm freight to Yeovil Junction, whilst the wagons on the front of the engine were to form the 8.22pm freight to Westbury which I was going to leave in the yard loop to be collected by a locomotive from Yeovil Town Loco later in the evening.

I had spoken to the signalman and had agreed the shunting moves, we moved up into the loop, where I detached the wagons from the front of the locomotive, and after screwing down the handbrake in the ex GWR 'Toad' brakevan at the rear of the Westbury goods, climbed onto the locomotive footplate and gave the go ahead for Joe Swaffield the driver to push on out to the long siding where I would join the 6.10pm to Yeovil Junction up to await its guard.

We started to propel out, the locomotive was not going very well, so I suggested to Joe that he 'gave her a bit more' which he did, but it did not make any difference. Suddenly the fireman reported 'there is a red light out here'. After telling Joe to stop I climbed down from the footplate and walked into the darkness, and found that we had three wagons off the road and they were fouling the main line, one of the wagons was sideways on, no wonder the locomotive was struggling!

I walked to the signalbox, and found that the signalman, worried that our shunting move was going to delay the 16.15 Taunton-Yeovil passenger train due off Hendford at 17.22, had shut us in by putting back the signal (ground disc) and opened the trap points. I also had a few words to the signalman about changing his mind, before he had to inform a platform full of people, mostly workers from the nearby Westland Aircraft factory that they were going to be late for tea! Then he had to get some buses organised. The oncoming train had to propel back from Montacute to Martock to run around (how times change) and return to Taunton.

Meanwhile there was nothing else for us to do except put the kettle on and await the arrival of the breakdown vans from Yeovil Town Shed which duly arrived behind a 'River' 2-6-0 with Driver Trevor Hayward at the controls. The funny thing is that whenever I had to send for the 'vans' to assist with a derailment, it was always Trevor Hayward who seemed to be driving the locomotive when they arrived. The wagons were re-railed and the track repaired with everything back to normal about 2.00am.

I had a visit a couple of days later from the District Inspector the late Ted Tolley from Templecombe which was itself a very important place in those days. He listened to my story, and said I would have to take the blame for not checking the ground signal, however, now I had 'come off the road' was now a proper shunter. The Inspector also went to have a quiet word with the signalman, and told him that, once a move is agreed with the shunter 'don't change your mind' a similar incident today would not be treated so lightly.

Old Joe knew the road
From Yatton to Yate
But even old Joe
Forgot Westland's Gate

So went the rhyme from the pen of Eric Reeve's after the argument between the aforementioned gate and our 57xx Pannier tank as we travelled to shunt in the private siding of Westland Aircraft one afternoon.

We went up the branch line to Westland's siding every day, sometimes twice, dependent on traffic flows to and from the works. On this particular day, we came out of the yard and up to the signal box at Hendford Halt where I collected the Annetts key to unlock the Westland ground frame thereby preventing the release of any tokens for the branch line.

We made our way along the single line to the ground frame, driver, fireman and two shunters (Eric and I) on the footplate of the pannier tank. Upon arrival at the ground frame I climbed down from the locomotive and unlocked and operated the ground frame switching the points for our entry into the siding.

I climbed back onto the locomotive and instructed Joe to proceed as far as the gate protecting the siding, which as we were a bit early, was not yet opened. The regulator was opened and we moved off.

Railwaymen who can remember Joe will know that he used to like to have a clean backhead on the boiler, and was always wiping it down with an oily rag, meanwhile, Eric and the fireman the late Ken Fay plus myself were talking together and not taking much notice of events, when there was a great yell from the ground. I shouted 'whoa' and looked over the side to see the siding gate hanging over the front of the locomotive! Harry Male the Westland employee was actually walking along the siding with the keys in his hand to unlock the padlock on the gate which was now hanging on the front of the pannier tank, unfortunately the gate wasn't much use after that!

The state of the track in Westland's siding was somewhat precarious and our locomotive dared not leave the headshunt upon entering, the aircraft company had their own engine for shunting on their rails namely a Howard 4-wheel chain driven diesel looking somewhat like a farm tractor on a huge bogie with a huge cab and crewed by Harry Male and a guy nicknamed 'Daisy' so called because he always had one in his mouth!

Another incident occurred at Westland's siding one afternoon, we had gone up there with four long wheelbase 'Tube' wagons on the rear of the locomotive, the wagons were to be loaded with helicopter rotor blades. Unfortunately the works engine did not have the power to drag the wagons from the rear of our locomotive and up the steep grade into the works.

It was Eric's idea for our locomotive to 'knock' the wagons up the grade, so it was time to flip the coupling off the engine drawbar and shout out 'hit them up Joe' which the driver duly did, unfortunately long wheelbase wagons and the state of the private siding track did not mix, with the result that all of the wagons are now off the road, and our locomotive is blocked in due to one of the wagons fouling our exit route back on to the branch line.

Harry told us not to worry, as he will fetch the mobile crane from the works and the wagons will be soon back on the rails, 'you railway blokes' go up to the canteen and have a cup of tea, as the job shouldn't take too long.

It was time for the fireman to fill up the boiler to keep the engine quite, screw the handbrake down, and driver, fireman, Eric and myself sit in the works canteen enjoying a cup of tea and a doughnut plus a cigarette whilst having a good natter, we are sitting there enjoying life, when this man comes in and asks 'any of you blokes railwaymen? 'They are ringing up about you, something about a train at Martock!

Crikey, we look at the clock, which was showing almost 4.00pm, time has flown by, and we had forgotten the Taunton - Yeovil passenger train. The Hendford signalman could not release the single-line token from Martock signal box because the Westland's ground frame is still open with the Annetts key still in the lock.

I have to run down and shut the frame and take the key back to Hendford box in order to release the passenger train from Martock. Eric had to take the can for this incident, and for the next few days we do the job properly, unlock the ground frame, engine into Westlands siding, lock frame, key back to signal box, then when shunting finished, fetch key from box, loco out of siding and key back to box, too much walking and hassle and soon returned to the old way of working.

One last incident that seemed hilarious at the time involved the whisky wagon. I was on early shift (04.40-16.40) and Eric on late (08.30-20.30) The local brewery Messrs Bruttons used to have a wagon of whisky and other spirits delivered once a week to Hendford yard via Taunton to be delivered to the brewery by railway lorry and this particular day was the whisky wagon day.

The driver, fireman and myself were having breakfast in the shunters cabin in Hendford yard, all railwaymen can remember the 'black hole' as it was known with its coal stove, gas lamp and piles of old coats on the wooden benches. Eric came on duty at 8.30am had a cup of tea and told me that 'he would go up with the locomotive to the long siding and bring in some wagons for unloading, and also would knock back the wagon off the Taunton goods for the shed 'you have the brake'. Fair enough. You have to bear in mind that the wagon would be rolling along at a fair speed as the far end of the yard was about ½ mile away, nothing to worry about as we had done it many times before, as long as I am there to apply the wagon brake hard enough to slow it down and enter the goods shed gently.

Eric meanwhile sets off up the yard with the locomotive, whilst I reckon I have time to use the toilet next door, whilst 'having the call of nature' I hear the familiar noise of wheels travelling over the rail joints and a box van passes by the toilet window at a fair pace approximately 150 yards from the goods shed, there is the sound of a terrific crash as the wagon sails into the empty goods shed hits the stop blocks at the far end and recoils out from the shed where I have time to grab the brake, shout a warning into the shed and walk calmly into the shed with the wagon again and stop it against the blocks, the wagon meanwhile smells strongly of whisky with liquid dripping onto the sleepers.

The door from the goods office opens, and out comes Charlie Hawkins the yard foreman complete with gold braid on his hat, a veteran railwayman, he was not amused. 'You b*****s have done it this time, you had better get Eric and get yourselves down here, quick. I walk up to the signal box nearly ½ mile away and explain the situation to Eric.

We return to the goods shed and enter the office and situated behind the stop blocks was the chief clerks desk, one Mr Cornelius and above his desk were shelves of files, some probably not disturbed from Brunel's day and many of these had deposited themselves and volumes of dust over his person, the other clerks were dusting him down and muttering vengeful thoughts about us, quite a costly incident and a wicked waste of spirit. Eric made out his usual multi-page report which really only said I was obeying a 'call of nature' and nothing more was heard.

Hendford was a traders yard, wagons had to be positioned for loading and unloading, and there was no room to manoeuvre easily unlike Yeovil Junction for example, which was a marshalling yard. The shunters from the junction if they had to come to Hendford to cover for sickness or holidays would get into a right tangle.

I well remember my late father in law - Ron Hawkins getting into a fair mess one day, insisting that he was the head shunter and I had to catch the brakes and change points. The yard foreman Charlie Hawkins had to tactfully ask him to let me sort it out when the workers came back from lunch to find that their wagons were not in position.

The traders Messrs Burts, Bradfords, Esso Petroleum, Co-op coal, Silcocks, Levers, Lyons Tea, Castrol Oil, all had their own private sidings or store sheds in the yard and many other companies such as Woolworths received wagon freight continuously, nowadays it all goes by road transport. The only people better off today are the residents of Rustywell mobile home park who used to complain about the 5.00am shunting - how times have changed.

When I drive down that way nowadays I can hardly believe all that work happened in Hendford yard, there were many more such incidents that were part and parcel of something that is sadly lacking today - good railway work! We were proud to be railwaymen back then. I have worked on the railway as a signalman at Yeovil Pen Mill for the past 17 years until retirement in 2005 but it is a very different game today, in fact a driver of many years whom I know was told by his manager that 'enjoying' was not in his job description - how sad.

Thankyou Mike for reliving shunting days at Hendford Goods.

For us, it is time to depart at 7.15 as the guard is waving his green flag, so with a blast on the loco whistle we pull away from the platform with a sharp bark from our exhaust, this sound eases as the reverser is pulled back, the regulator eased, then opened again as we head towards Montacute.

The advanced starting signal has its arm lowered ahead of us as we pass the vast works of Westland Helicopters standing on our right and its network of rail sidings including the connection with the branch line.

We are striding up a small gradient as we pass under Bunford lane overbridge, and I grab the firing shovel, open the bunker flap and place some more coal into the firebox, mostly under the firedoor, the glare from the fire is almost blinding, plus the heat making rivulets of sweat run down my face, with the bout of firing ceasing for the moment, I shut the bunker flap and place the shovel back into the corner of the cab.

The cab of the locomotive is shaking and rattling, with the fire beating and dancing in time with the exhaust beats from our chimney, and the needles of the steam and vacuum gauges quivering in their brass cases, reverser in almost mid gear and regulator half open as we near the top of Montacute bank.

I put the injector on in order to keep the boiler level up as we approach the summit and start running downhill picking up speed. My mate eases the regulator and moves the reverser forward as we will run under our own momentum from here.

We enter a large cutting passing under two magnificent overbridges, built originally by the Bristol and Exeter Railway to encompass broad gauge track, the cutting is wide as it was designed to take a double broad gauge line, although only one line of track was ever laid. The bridges however still stand in the 21st century and now cover a roadway instead of railway track.

As we rattle down the bank I lean over the side of the cab puffing on a woodbine and taking advantage of the fresh air, our connecting rods are a fast blur, with our driving wheels spinning madly, smoke and steam billow from the chimney, the injector is just stopping the safety valves from lifting as the demand for steam decreases.

I always liked this cutting, it was a haven for wildlife, rabbits, foxes, badgers all could be seen here at various times, including the banks covered with wild primroses in spring time.

A.E.West

Hendford Goods Junction looking towards Yeovil Town, the tracks on the left lead into Hendford Goods.

Hendford Goods yard, the small brick building to the left, is the shunters cabin, known to everyone as the 'black hole' due to the combined atmosphere of cigarette smoke and 'fry ups'.

A.E.West

Shunting days at Hendford, from the left Mike Herrin (shunter), Nigel Extance (fireman), Eric Reeves (leading shunter) stand in front of U class 2-6-0 31792 in Hendford Goods yard.

Mike Herrin

Ex LSWR bogie rail wagon No.DS64558 viewed here at Hendford Goods on 18 February 1965 - built by Cravens of Sheffield for the LSWR, one of 14 constructed and delivered in 1902. Wagon length 47' 6" long, to carry 45ft long rails which were introduced in 1903, this must have been the last survivor as it was seen again by Ted West later in 1965. Wagon colour black with red side rails. *A.E West*

Pannier tank 9754 takes a break from shunting duties at Hendford Goods on 18 February 1965. I bet I know where the crew are – having a cup of tea in the shunters cabin. *A.E.West*

Hendford Goods shed was 150ft long, contained three 30cwt cranes, and held seven wagons. This was the scene of Mike Herrin's rough shunt with the whisky wagon! *A.E.West*

The wooden waiting shelter complete with gas lamp at Hendford Halt on 18 February 1965, passenger services had ceased in June of the previous year.   *A.E.West*

Hendford Halt signal box situated opposite the Halt platform was opened by 1881, a fire caused damage on 25 June 1926, with the roof being replaced by a GWR standard design timber top, equipped with a 24-lever frame the box closed on 12 September 1965.   *A.E.West*

A view taken on 18 February 1965 of the rear of Hendford signal box showing Westlands siding in the distance and the trackwork leading towards Montacute, all of the structure and signalling is intact, despite the fact, that passenger services had stopped running since 15 June 1964.   *A.E.West*

Westland Aircraft Works situated in an ideal rural location, from a postcard dated 1927, the branch line with plenty of freight wagons in attendance can be seen running the whole length of the factory, Hendford Halt would not open until 2 May 1932. The comparison with the same area today, could not be more remarkable.   *Authors Collection*

The GWR branch line stands in the background in this official works photograph of a Fowler 0-4-0 diesel mechanical locomotive in Westland's Works siding on 11 March 1932. The locomotive fitted with a Petters 'ACE' three cylinder engine, and subsequently named *ACE* was purchased in 1931 and in true GWR tradition painted green with a copper chimney cap for the exhaust.

Institute of Agricultural History and Museum of English Rural Life, University of Reading

Having breasted the top of Montacute bank, No.4663 runs down towards Hendford Halt with the 12.58 from Taunton on 24 March 1962.

John Day

The Station Master, his staff and passengers pose for posterity on the platform of Montacute station pre 1908, the platform mounted signal box opened on 6 March of that year will be located on the platform to the left of the station building. A wonderful array of gas lamps occupies the length of the platform.

Unknown photographer–Malcolm Evans Collection

An indistinct but important photograph of Montacute, showing the ground mounted signalbox on the left hand side past the signal, this box standing opposite the goods shed and dating from 1882 was replaced by a signal box located on the station platform from 6 March 1908.

Unknown photographer-Malcolm Evans Collection

A 2-6-2T calls at Montacute bunker first with a Taunton to Yeovil train in 1962. Upper quadrant signals have now replaced the GWR lower quadrant arms. The station masters house on the right, now stands alongside the busy A3088 link road between the A303 at Cartgate and Yeovil.

Peter Barnfield

Peter Barnfield

Montacute looking towards Martock in 1962. The posts on the right for the single line tokens, hardly being used as the 13 lever frame signal box was often switched out, eventually closing on 8 March 1964. The station which had opened in 1882 closed on 15 June 1964

The Bristol & Exeter station building at Martock, the corrugated building on the platform was installed by the GWR to 'increase parcel accommodation' for the sum of £100 in 1905.

Authors Collection

With the closure of the line, certain sections were used for training civil engineering staff during the winter of 1964/65; pictured near East Street Drove Crossing is a Plassermatic Tamping Machine used for packing ballast.

Patrick Palmer

Martock signalman Tom Howell exchanges single line tokens with the fireman of 82044 on a Yeovil – Taunton train. . The large hoop is for the section to Langport West, and the brass baton for the section from Hendford, the fireman has the injector turned on to top up the boiler, the tender sprinklers to keep the coal dust down, can be seen in action at the rear top of the cab

John Cornelius

A passenger train from Taunton hauled by 82044 trundles over the level crossing at Martock heading for Yeovil on 16 May 1964.

John Cornelius

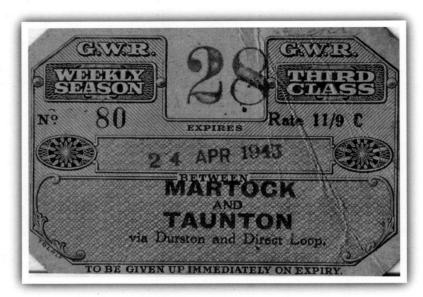

A GWR third class weekly season ticket issued on 24 April 1943 at a cost of 11/9 between Martock and Taunton. *Collection Malcolm Evans*

The signalman leans out of his box at Martock to exchange single line tokens with the fireman of large prairie No.6157 working a Taunton-Yeovil service on 28 April 1962.

R.S.Carpenter/P.J.Garland Collection

Signal box and level crossing at Martock viewed from the down platform in 1962, the gates on the left protect the entrance to the up goods yard. Electric lighting was supplied to the station and signal box in 1945 for £135.

Peter Barnfield

The up platform at Martock was supplied with an attractive wooden waiting shelter, 4656 approaches with a Taunton to Yeovil train in 1962.
Peter Barnfield

Having picked up passengers for Yeovil, 4656 approaches Martock signalbox with the signalman already holding the brass baton for the Martock-Hendford single line section in 1962. Passengers from the train who have alighted and crossed the footbridge now walk along the down platform to the station exit.
Peter Barnfield

Pannier tanks cross at Martock, No 4656 on the left with a Taunton-Yeovil train in 1962, the fireman of the Yeovil-Taunton service on the right, is either watering down the coal with the pep pipe, or cracking lumps of coal. Martock and Langport West were the only crossing places for passenger trains on the branch.

Peter Barnfield

MONTACUTE

We are braking hard now as we pass the Montacute distant signal, and upon reflection I remember that of all the stations between Yeovil Town and Langport West. Montacute was the only station to have moveable distant signals, all of the others had their distant arms permanently fixed at caution.

The signal box here was usually switched out, and mostly came into use when the Monday – Friday goods train from Taunton required to pick up and drop off wagons, this was worked in 1963 under Plymouth Duty No.834 using Taunton footplatemen (WX) booked using a 2-6-2 BR Standard tank departing from Taunton at 6.20am with an arrival at Pen Mill of 9.35am departing at 10.10 shunting at all stations and arriving in Taunton at 2.40pm.

More braking now as we coast in with regulator closed and run past the goods shed and cattle dock and stop at the platform, which is on my side of the cab. This station serving the beautiful village of Montacute was my favourite on the whole branch, it was the epitome of a GWR branch line station with its distinctive station building complete with small signal box on the platform, this opened in 1908 replacing an earlier signal box standing opposite the goods shed.

The station did not open with the line in 1853 opening instead in 1882 although it was not the last station to appear on the branch as Hendford Halt opened in 1932.

The goods shed was served by a single siding with points at either end, with the point at the Hendford end being operated by a two-lever ground frame, which was released by the single line staff. A small cattle dock at the Hendford end of the platform was served by a head shunt of the goods shed siding.

As the station is on my side of the cab, it is my turn to lean out of the cab and look for the 'right away'

CLARENCE JOHN BRADLEY RECALLS MONTACUTE STATION

'The voice of the stationmaster calling '*Montacute*' resounded around the station as my train slowed down and eventually came to a halt at the platform. Alighting from the train I made my way to the station exit beneath the soft glow of the gas lamp which hung from its bracket by the signal box.

Whilst handing in my ticket I stood and watched the fireman shovelling in coal to the hungry flames of the engine's firebox. The fingers of flame illuminated the footplate showing the image of the drivers' face intent on his business of watching the gauges and instruments while wiping his hands with some cotton waste. The stationmaster blew his whistle and with a hiss of steam and a rattle of couplings the train proceeded on its journey.

Walking up the hill I crossed the bridge where Wellhams Brook gurgled on its way to the flour mill at Stoke-Sub-Hambdon. The hedges each side of the line were very high, their branches menacingly reaching out to the night sky.

Montacute station in daylight beheld a different scene entirely. There was a coming and going of the merchant's coal lorries whose offices were situated on the right hand side of the entrance gates. I remember distinctly going into the wooden office to be confronted by a clerk sitting on a high stool at a desk and peering over the top of his glasses questioning my presence. My reply being to order some coal and have it delivered.

The sun shone through the grimy window, its shaft of light showing particles of dust on the desk, whereupon the clerk picked up a pen and dipped it into the inkwell and, with the pen nib scratching the paper, dutifully completed the order. Coming out of the office, my eye met with the cattle pens where the animals were secured awaiting delivery to the nearest market.

The station was built with hamstone, had tall chimneys and a slate roof. The canopy over the platform was enhanced with ornate finials that blended with the hanging baskets of flowers. The waiting room with its ticket office adjoining saw many different faces of passengers over the years, some peering at the now forgotten posters advertising holidays and chocolate products.

Standing on the platform awaiting the arrival of the train you may have perceived the flower garden festooned with bright flowers, and in comparison the oily and stained ballast supporting the shiny railway lines. Walking up the station yard you passed a large grey painted, hand operated crane, which was used for loading and uploading trucks parked on the sidings. The goods were stored in a capacious shed at the end of the yard. This shed was in constant use with storing of grain and other perishable products. In latter years it housed a pair of barn owls which glided ghostly around the now derelict yard in search of food.

At the time for harvesting sugar beet the station yard seemed besieged with trailers and horse and carts laden with beet. Sound of beet being loaded into the empty trucks echoed throughout the yard in the early morning frost. The men loading the trucks were clad in overcoats and leather jerkins; some blew lustily on their fingernails while others stamped their feet on the ground to restore circulation. I have seen whole lines of trucks laden with sugar beet awaiting collection for the refinery, which proved that Montacute Station served the village and the farming community to its fullest ability.'

MALCOLM EVANS - HAPPY MEMORIES OF MONTACUTE

'My memories of the Taunton-Yeovil line from the 1950s and early 1960s always commenced in the North East of England when my parents, two brothers, sister and I commenced our journey at Middlesborough around 7.00pm and travelling via Darlington would travel overnight to Bristol Temple Meads station, arriving just after 5am.

Tired and weary after staying awake throughout the journey collecting train numbers, we would depart from Bristol around 6.45am for the journey to Taunton arriving there at approximately 8.20am.

The train for Yeovil usually formed of three coaches would be standing in the up bay on platform 9, there was no sign of a locomotive, as this would be attached later.

We board the train and enter a non-corridor compartment coach, this had long bench seats on either side, which I remember when wearing shorts, always made my legs itch as they were filled with horse hair.

A mirror and photographs above the seats displaying views of the West Country, and brown leather straps on each door to open and close the window were all part of travelling by train in those days.

The carriage cleaners are busy with buckets of water and long handled brushes to clean the windows and exterior of the carriage, a slight bump is felt afterwards, as the locomotive a small prairie 2-6-2 tank couples to our train just before departure time of 9.45am.

After stopping at Athelney, Langport West, and Thorney & Kingsbury Halt we enter Martock where we pass the 10.19am departure for Taunton, this will be another number to note down, departing Martock at 10.22am we soon view from our carriage window the familiar sight of St. Michael's tower in the distance.

Time to pull ourselves together, and to the sound of '*Montacute*' '*Montacute*' we arrive at our destination, my father lets the window down by its heavy leather strap, opens the door and complete with our luggage step down onto the platform.

I stand and watch as the guard blows his whistle, with a return call from the locomotive as it barks away into the distance towards Yeovil.

After having our tickets examined by the porter its time for the long walk from the station into Station road down the hill and up the other side into the village, eventually arriving at my grandmothers house in Townsend to the sound of the church clock striking after a journey of nearly sixteen hours.

Compared to the stations surrounded by industry in the North East where I grew up- Montacute station was tranquil and peaceful, it had a ticket/parcels office, waiting room, ladies and gents toilets and a small signal office near the station exit leading into a small goods yard. I also recall the name of Montacute marked out in white painted stones on the bank side opposite the platform.

During a visit to my Aunt in Yeovil in May 1962 by train hauled by large prairie tank No. 6113 my brother and I decided to visit the locomotive shed at Yeovil Town Station 72C. Upon arrival at the station we crossed the platforms via the footbridge and entered the shed area by a small Iron Gate.

After receiving permission to have a look around, we noted the following locomotives on shed that day; 3733, 4507, 30667, 31632, 34033 *Chard*. 34075 *264 Squadron* and 76067. M7 30129 was standing in the station with the push-pull to Yeovil Junction.

My last journey on the line was in May 1963 (a year before closure) we were pulled by small prairie tank No 4591 on the 9.45am from Taunton to Montacute and the same locomotive hauled us from Montacute to Yeovil Pen Mill a few days later for a visit to my Aunt in Yeovil.

I remember at Yeovil Town station looking from the carriage window and glimpsing a small pannier tank No.5410 with auto-coach W240W working the push & pull service to Yeovil Junction, plus Bulleid Pacific No.34007 *Wadebridge* on shed.

For our last return journey along the line we were hauled by BR Standard 3MT tank 82042 in green livery working the 10.12am from Montacute arriving into platform 1 at Taunton at 10.52am and the long journey north.

It was through the encouragement of my father and grandfather who both worked on the railway in the North East of England that inspired me to join the railway, working at Thornaby, Gloucester (Barnwood), and Eastleigh as a locomotive fireman and also on the Permanent Way department at Yeovil Junction'.

WYNDHAM PALMER – PHEASANTS AT MONTACUTE

'After working at Thorney Halt for a few years I transferred to Montacute as a porter signalman. The man before me had lived in the station house, which had become vacant, and as I was getting married, put in for the house and was fortunate to get it.

The job was a jack of all trades, and I did everything including; booking office, with its monthly and weekly bookings, signalman, shunter, cleaner, filling the signal lamps, everything.

There was one siding which held coal traffic, plus sugar beet when in season and incoming loads of seed potatoes, the goods shed was rented out to the Somerset & Dorset Box Company from Yeovil, the station was under the control of the station master at Martock Mr Cousins. I operated the signal box for the daily goods from Taunton and used to switch the box in with the permission of Martock and Hendford boxes, the switching in gear was unusual as it was made of brass. The box interior was kept in an immaculate condition, the brass work being cleaned every day.

Mondays was lamp day, and there were about 7 or 8 signal lamps to change, after the goods train had left for Yeovil, I walked up through the cutting to replace the oil lamp in the down distant signal, this was about a half mile walk and I used to keep an eye out for any pheasants that had been knocked down by the preceding train, and if they were not too bad, they would make a good meal, I would also pick wild strawberries.

When the line closed I worked in the Yeovil Town parcels office until closure.

Thank you Clarence, Malcolm and Wyndham for your recollections.

We have the guards green flag at our departure time of 7.24 and we are on our way again with our engine getting into its stride and gathering speed as we skirt the grounds of Montacute House built during the 1590s by Sir Edward Phelips, Speaker of the House of Commons.

This magnificent house which at one time once brought many distinguished visitors to the station over the years, is under the custodianship of the National Trust and well worth a visit.

The pre-cast concrete sections that once supported Montacute station platform can now be found in use at Doniford Halt on the West Somerset Railway.

The maximum permitted load for our class of locomotive (45XX) between Yeovil and Durston was 270 tons, but with our 'B'set coaches rolling along behind us we are well within the limit. Blue group locomotives working to a limit of 330 tons were permitted over the branch during the Second World War, working ambulance and munitions trains.

Meanwhile we continue onwards to Martock, with our engine running like a sewing machine with an even beat from our exhaust, the vacuum pump slapping away in fine style, time to check the fire as I open the firedoors, the heat reflects sharply into the enclosed cab, as by holding the firing shovel just inside the firebox and deflecting the blade, it is possible to see where the next shovels of coal have to be placed.

I leave the firedoors open and raise the firing flap, then dig the shovel into the bunker, swing around and pull down the firing flap by its chain, then place the shovel of coal into the firebox, exactly where needed, close the flap, dig into the bunker and so on until firing requirements are met.

The injector is put on again to keep the boiler topped up, and a quick swill with the pep pipe around the cab floor to keep the coal dust down, careful of course not to splash my mates boots.

The injector is still singing away pumping water into the boiler as the Martock fixed distant signal appears ahead of us, my mate closes the regulator and pulls hard on the whistle chain with the sharp note from our whistle resounding around the countryside.

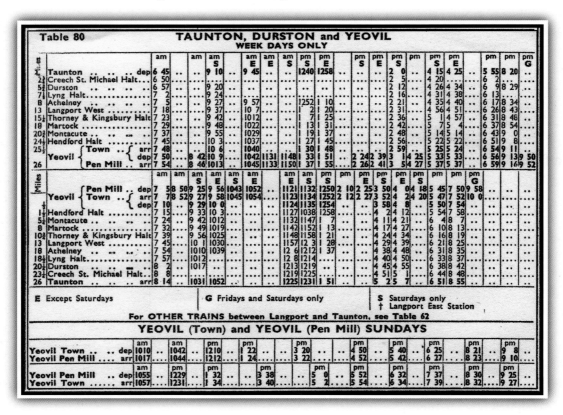

MARTOCK TO CURRY RIVEL JUNCTION

MARTOCK

The vacuum brake is being applied and we start to slow, as ahead of us the outer and inner home signal arms are lowered and road vehicles can be seen standing at the level crossing gates awaiting our passage.

A plume of steam is rising from the locomotive standing alongside the up platform, this is the 6.45 am Taunton to Yeovil Pen Mill crewed by Taunton men with a booked arrival at Pen Mill of 7.54.

Taunton men had reported on shed at 6.00am for Duty No.33 which in 1963 was usually rostered to a BR 2-6-2T. After arrival at Pen Mill the Taunton engine would be used for shunting duties including a trip to Yeovil Town and return to Pen Mill before departing Yeovil with the 9.56am passenger train to Taunton.

Martock pronounced 'Mardik' in the local vernacular had a staggered platform layout with the down platform containing the main platform building and the up platform just had a basic wooden shelter, a footbridge connected both platforms.

The signal box stands alongside the up line to our right as we approach still braking over the level crossing, the signalman is standing ready alongside the track with the hoop for the section to Langport West in his upraised hand.

The signalman has already received the single line token from the Taunton fireman and has cleared the section ahead to Langport for us, whilst our token which I have just surrendered to the signalman will clear the section onwards to Hendford for the 6.45 ex Taunton.

From Martock to Langport West we have reverted to the large steel hoop containing the token in its pouch. Martock was always a well patronised station, and no exception on this day as with a booked arrival in Taunton at 8.14am this is a good train for workers and school children alike, also for the main line connections at Taunton.

The platform is on my side of the cab as we come to a halt with a screeching of brakes from our coaches, passengers move forward and join our train, plus the sound of heavy coach doors slamming shut, hustle and bustle from the station staff as they load and unload parcel traffic at the luggage van at the rear of our train.

There is a crackle of an exhaust, plus a blast on the whistle and the rumble of coaches as the 6.45 ex Taunton pulls away alongside us at 07.29 on the way to Yeovil, the signalman leaning out of the his box window handing the single line token to the fireman as the Yeovil bound train barks its way across the level crossing and the next stop at Montacute.

Signal arms return to danger in the wake of the departing train with the sound of its exhaust beat growing fainter in the distance, the level crossing gates controlled by the signalman open to road traffic behind our train, the heavy gates coming together with a bang across the tracks.

The railway layout here is quite impressive for a branch line station with the main goods yard being located on the down side, the goods shed is 50ft long and contains a 2 ton hand operated crane, 21 freight wagons can be accommodated on the goods shed road.

The shunting neck holds 25 wagons and the three roads between the goods shed and the gas works siding hold 11, 17 & 18 wagons respectively. The crane road behind the up platform - 24 wagons. Goods inwards included; coal for local traders and the gasworks, timber, building materials, agricultural machinery, horses and cattle.

Due to a catch point in the up platform loop being situated 202 yards to the rear of the up inner home signal, and before up freight trains of more than 26 wagons plus engine and brake van were allowed to enter the station, the up inner home signal had to be lowered, in order for the train to run as far as the signal box, thus clearing the catch point.

If a passenger train was of such a length, that it stopped with its rear section over the catch point, the Station Master was responsible for clipping the point until the train was clear.

Local passenger traffic was good, and I well remember working the summer Sunday School excursions to Weymouth, and the platform would be full of families.

The branch was normally closed on Sundays except for the milk traffic from Thorney, and the signal boxes at Martock and Hendford would be opened for the passenger specials, for which services the carriages would be brought over from Yeovil Town by one of our U class 2-6-0s and then taken to Pen Mill and onwards to Weymouth crewed by Yeovil footplatemen.

Another service worked from Martock at least a couple of times a week or when required, involved one of our pannier tank engines travelling light engine over from Yeovil plus a guard who would travel on the footplate with us.

At Martock we would collect a wagon with a refrigerated container holding meat from the local abattoir and complete with brakevan would return to Yeovil Pen Mill where the wagon would be attached to an up service.

A private siding agreement between the Martock & District Gas Consumers Ltd and the Great Western Railway dated from December 1898. This meant revenue for the Railway Company in delivering wagon loads of coal, plus tripping the empties back to Taunton for marshalling onwards to South Wales.

PAM WHITE - MEMORIES OF MARTOCK GASWORKS

'You would have thought that, being brought up in the country, you would look out from your bedroom window and view green pastures, clothed with sheep, and breathe in pure air – not so for the children of Newtown when the Martock Gas Company made coal gas. Our landscape was one of industry and much of our childhood lives revolved around the Gasworks and Bradfords yard and the air was certainly not pure!

A whiff of Carbon Monoxide was never far away! Added to this, metal wheelbarrows loaded with shimmering red hot coke, were trundled by the stokers from the retort house to the coke yard where they were emptied and doused with water, which made for smelly acrid fumes. Nevertheless I loved being allowed to 'swoosh' the water and watch as the red embers turned grey.

Other thought provoking smells came from the Great Western Railway engines that puffed in and out of Martock station and then there was the burning of sawdust at Hebditch's Works. The railway siding was a very important link to the gasworks, and here the tar (another by product) was pumped from a nearby 'tar well' into a railway tanker and hauled away. If I remember rightly, this job was done by a man called Jimmy Carter who lived in one of the row of cottages in North Street almost opposite what was then the Methodist Church.

I am not quite sure what a small girl with pigtails was doing in the heart of the gas works, but I often used to watch the procedure. I suppose because the works was virtually just outside our small back yard that is where I 'played'. Besides this, we enjoyed a freedom unknown today. At the same time it seemed a perfectly normal thing to do.

I used to tip toe my way over puddles through a steamy, hissing, covered walkway to the Retort House, known to us as the 'Stoke Hole' to watch the stokers extracting almost white hot coke from the furnaces with long iron 'L' shaped rakes. It was difficult and dangerous work and the stoker's hands were often burnt and became calloused and hard.

Two gasholders were located approximately 30 yards from the side of the Gas House, now called Radiant House, where we lived. On occasions, when it was evident that German bombers were flying overhead on their way to blitz Bristol, with their unmistakable throb of engines, my parents insisted that Granny and my sister Val and I should sit cooped up under the stairs.

With the gasholders so near, I used to think to myself 'we might as well stay in bed' if they decided to drop any bombs. One was in fact dropped near Coat Bridge.

Children would arrive at the coke yard on Saturday mornings with all sorts of innovative home-made carts, or maybe an old pram, to collect a sack of coke, which was used in many of our homes. We certainly didn't have central heating, huddling instead around a fire which, on wet Mondays, was shared with a clothes horse of steaming washing.

The Gas Company owned one lorry and one van. The driver of the lorry was Mr Len Westlake (Pam Mabers dad). I travelled many miles on a cushion wedged on top of the handbrake between Len and my dad, Alex Handcock. One day we went to the other side of the world (or so it seemed) to pick up a gas engine – actually it was Sidmouth.

The street lighting in Martock, South Petherton, Norton, Stoke and Montacute was by gas lamp. Once a week my dad and I went by van to each of these villages to wind up the clock timers and light any of the pilot lights that had blown out. Dad wore a bowler hat for this job! It was quite tiring, shinning up and down a ladder, at the end of a busy week.

Sunday was an important day for the gas works – 'Blunderbuss', a huge gas engine, had to be started to pump enough gas around the district to cook all the Sunday roasts. The noise it made could be heard reverberating all over the village. A small engine called 'Dinky' was started every weekday at 4.30pm, for the same reason, to cook everyone's evening meal. When I was old enough I was taught how to crank Dinky into life – remembering to open all the oil valves. Perhaps I should have learnt to sew instead!

Thankyou Pam for your excellent recollections, informing us that village life is not all roses around the door etc.

JILL CLARK - TRAVELLING TO HENDFORD HALT FROM MARTOCK

'I used to catch the train from Martock in the morning and travel to Hendford Halt as I worked at Westland's, unfortunately after finishing work each night at 5.00pm, there was no return train service until 5.54pm from Hendford, so I returned to Martock by bus, except on Tuesdays and Fridays when it travelled via Long Load.

On Tuesdays and Fridays I used to walk to Yeovil Town station and get the 5.50pm train to Martock, this was a useful service, as I had typing lessons on Friday and they finished in time for me to catch the train. There was one engine driver that would not leave Martock until all of his regular morning passengers were on board the train. I remember being late one morning, and he noticed me hurrying by the ticket office and waited until I was safely aboard.

Saturday was a favourite day out for me to go shopping in Taunton by train; my father frequently travelled on the train from Martock as he also worked at Westland's.

The train was cheaper than the bus – and much quicker'.

Thankyou Jill for your recollections, and how stations such as Martock were a vital lifeline for passengers travelling to work.

PATRICK PALMER – MEMORIES OF HORSES AT MARTOCK STATION.

'During the agricultural depression of the 1930's my father, Arthur Palmer, always going by train from Martock Station, started to go regularly to Ireland, travel around the traditional Irish fairs and buy unbroken horses. He imported hundreds over the next 30 years, schooled and sold them usually for hunting.

They came over to England by boat to Fishguard or Holyhead and then travelled by train and arrived at Martock Station in excellent condition about half a dozen at a time. I well recall them being led up through Martock to Bower Hinton Farm, about 1½ miles. Try doing that today with 6 horses!

While returning from Ireland on one occasion he fell asleep between Thorney Halt and Martock eventually waking up in Montacute Station. Mother, who was still waiting in Martock, wasn't best pleased.

During the war when petrol was rationed we used to catch the train in Martock Station to go shopping in either Taunton or Yeovil, it was so easy. Those were the days of true public transport.

One-day aged about four while collecting horses at Martock, a steam engine was shunting goods wagons. The engine stopped right beside us on the platform and the driver asked if I would like a ride. Quick as a flash I climbed into his cab and off we went shunting for about 20 minutes. What a thrill for a child but of course it would never be allowed today. It probably wasn't then but with a war to fight, there were far more important things for officials to worry about!

After the railway had closed I was going past the level crossing as the signal box was being demolished. The nameplate 'Martock Signal Box' was still fixed to the front of the building and I decided to do something about it, and asked the man who had bought the signal box, if the nameplate could be purchased.

His reply being, that the nameplate was too valuable and would fetch a high price in London etc. Determined not to be persuaded by this argument, I then noticed that the demolition gang had to remove the long crossing sleepers which formed the floor of the signalbox and place them on to their lorry, this presented them with a problem as they had no lifting equipment. During the 1960's mechanical diggers were not a common sight in the area. However. I did have a digger at my farm in Bower Hinton and agreed with the man that I would fetch it and load the long crossing sleepers on to their lorry, providing he gave me the nameplate, this was duly accomplished, the deal was struck and I became the owner of the Martock signal box nameplate, happy in the knowledge that something tangible with the history of the Parish will always remain here.

I scraped off the green Southern Region paint from the nameplate, and restored it to its original colours of chocolate and cream, as when the GWR used to own and operate the line through the station.

The railway still lives on, as most of the ballast removed from the line when the railway closed, was used on farms around the Martock and Bower Hinton area as packing for trackways etc.'

Thankyou Patrick for your memories, and for your foresight in saving the nameplate from going elsewhere.

Whilst awaiting the 'right away' from our guard I have taken the chance for a few minutes to escape the heat of the cab and stand on the platform having another woodbine. I have already abandoned my overall jacket due to the temperature inside the cab, and am stood there in my black tee shirt, bib and brace overalls, with my black greaseproof cap at a jaunty angle on my head 'a boy fireman' without a worry in the world. Elvis Presley, Duane Eddy and the Everly Brothers being my heroes at the time (and still are).

My mate has come over to my side of the cab and leans out to see what is going on along the platform, our locomotive meanwhile is making her own noise, the steam blower has been turned on slightly to stop the flames and smoke drifting back into the cab, the firedoors are open, the fire is reflected against the back of the cab in contrast to the hot summer sunshine, and the noise of the vacuum ejector roaring through the chimney echoes along the platform.

Whisps of steam drift from the locomotive, from the cylinders and the safety valves, smoke drifts around the station from our chimney, no time for me to gawp around as the sound of the guards whistle resounds along the platform.

Time to climb aboard, shut the cab and firedoors, the station starting signal is off, my mate opens the regulator, there is a small delay until steam reaches the cylinders, with a sharp crack from the exhaust we pull away, the blast from the exhaust softens as the reverser is eased back by my mate, and by the time that the advanced starting signal is passed, we are cracking on, with the cab of the locomotive shaking and rolling as we head towards Thorney Halt.

The nature of the landscape now starts to change as we enter the flatlands of Somerset, home of the withie used in roof thatching, where statuesque herons hunt for fish in the network of rhines (pronounced as rheens) that drain the land, this is the most remote and beautiful part of Somerset, and relatively unspoilt to this day.

The station layout at Martock as viewed from the up platform in 1962.   *Peter Barnfield*

Thorney Milk Depot and siding is seen to the right as 82008 gets into her stride and heads towards Martock with a Taunton-Yeovil train on 8 February 1962. *John Cornelius*

The points leading into Thorney Milk Depot in the foreground as 4591 approaches Thorney & Kingsbury Halt on 20 May 1964. *John Cornelius*

Steam bellows from the clack valve on 4591 whilst standing at Thorney & Kingsbury Halt with a train for Taunton on 29 May 1964.

John Cornelius

With safety valves lifting 82042 arrives at Thorney & Kingsbury Halt on 29 May 1964 with a Taunton-Yeovil train.

John Cornelius

With a lightweight load behind her bunker, No.5798 trundles past Thorney milk depot with a pick-up goods for Langport West on 21 March 1962. *John Cornelius*

A scene of pride tempered with sadness as soldiers and their families await the train at Langport West Station in 1914. *Pam Rayne*

THORNEY & KINGSBURY HALT

As stations on the branch were not far apart, and providing the locomotive started its journey with a full firebox, it only needed the fireman to feed coal into the back corners and under the firedoor between stations to generate enough steam for the journey, although he couldn't be lax, as a rough trip, could appear at any moment on the footplate.

We jog along on the three mile run to Thorney and Kingsbury Halt to give it its proper name, but to all and sundry known as 'Thorney'.

A blast on the whistle as we approach the halt, no signals here, as we run past the Nestles milk depot which stands to our left and served by a loop off the branch, the points operated by two ground frames (north and south) released by the key on the single line token.

The single platform which was on my side of the locomotive was placed under the iron overbridge carrying the road from Kingsbury Episcopi to Muchelney over the railway, a small building contained the waiting room/ticket office.

Entrance to the Halt which opened on 28 November 1927 was via a small gate and a flight of wooden steps, oil lamps for illumination were provided at the top of the steps, plus two on the platform and two standing adjacent to the ground frames.

We screech to a stop alongside the platform and await passengers to board our train; smoke and steam billowing out from our chimney and drifting back under the roadbridge.

Glancing back along the platform I can see a few people climbing aboard, and after the last door has slammed shut, the sound of the guards whistle echoes under the bridge.

WYNDHAM PALMER – MEMORIES OF THORNEY

'After being appointed I used to catch the early train from Martock to start work, there was a small waiting room plus booking office situated on the platform underneath the road bridge.

Part of my job was to sell tickets to the public, which numbered 20-30 passengers per day, the other part of the job involved washing out the bogie siphon 'G's in the milk siding adjoining Thorney Halt. The milk came in by road from the local farms and 6 rail tanks plus 2 siphon 'G's went out per day, the siphons contained channel islands milk in 17 gallon churns. Nestles staff loaded the wagons and would give me the load notes, and I labelled the wagons.

I used to get on well with the dairy staff and used to have my dinner in their canteen and was made quite welcome, and knew most of the workers. I was my own boss; the halt came under the jurisdiction of the Martock stationmaster Mr Cousins. I would never see him from one month to the next. The job was wet and cold during the winter because of the constant washing out of the bogie siphons, I had a fire in the booking office to keep warm, and if it was smoky, it looked like, the whole bridge was on fire, and a car driver travelling along the road would see smoke billowing out from both sides of the bridge, this was caused by me trying to light the fire with paraffin.

Due to road transport, the daily output dropped from six rail trucks per day to one before closure. I used to catch the afternoon train back to Martock, after working at Thorney for two or three years I transferred to Montacute as a porter signalman.

Thankyou Wyndham.

Off we set again, injector off, regulator open and pull away to the last station on the branch which is about six minutes away, no need to tend to the firebox, which is full, and have ample steam without lifting the safety valves, the boiler is about three quarters full, and all is well, the beautiful Somerset countryside looks lush and green as I lean over the side of the cab puffing away on a cigarette.

Ahead of us we spot members of the permanent way staff standing alongside the trackside, a blast on the whistle to warn of our approach, has them holding their arms up in response as we pass, and as as we roll by, the branch line will resound into silence, and they can carry on with their maintenance.

The 'Motor Economic System' was installed on the Taunton branch in 1932/3 this system involved provision of a motorised trolley (or trolleys) in order that the permanent way gangs could cover a larger area therefore becoming more economic, hence the name of the system.

The provision of occupation keys permitted the gang to occupy a section when not required for the occupation of trains. When the occupation key was out, the electric train staff or token could not be obtained.

In order that the section could be cleared quickly when a train was due, occupation key boxes were installed at intervals through each block section, the ganger would return the key to the nearest one after clearing the line of the motorised trolley by use of a portable turntable. The signalman could then obtain a staff for the next train. This system was installed by the GWR on many of its longer branch lines.

We rattle through the ancient areas of Somerset, with only the passage of our train rattling across the moorland to disturb the peace and tranquillity of the Isle of Muchelney, and it is this peaceful and remote area that led to a monastery being established here in 939 by King Athelstan. The Abbey of Muchelney lasting until the dissolution in 1538.

	TAUNTON DUTY No. 33		
	3 P.T./3 F.T. (B.R. Standard)		
—	Taunton Loco. ...	... 6. 0 a.m. ‖	
6. 5 a.m.	Taunton	—	
	C—Shunting		
—	Taunton	... 6.45 a.m. P	
7.54 a.m.	Yeovil Pen Mill	—	
	C—Shunting 8.0 a.m. to 8.45 a.m.		
—	Yeovil Pen Mill ...	... 9.10 a.m. V	
9.12 a.m.	Yeovil Town ...	... 9.25 a.m. cpld	
		or E.B.V.	
9.29 a.m.	Yeovil Pen Mill ...	... 9.56 a.m. P	
10.53 a.m.	Taunton	...11. 0 a.m. ‖	
11. 5 a.m.	Taunton Loco.	—	
Taunton Men.			

LANGPORT WEST

All too soon the Langport West distant signal fixed at caution and standing 1,076 yards from the signal box appears ahead of us, a long blast on the whistle heralds our approach as the regulator is closed, and with injector on and with my mate applying the vacuum brake handle we coast pass the inner home signal.

The signal box is on my side of the cab standing off the end of the platform and I place the hooped token over the 'cows horn' receiving post for the signalman to collect.

We run along alongside the platform with the solid slap of the vacuum pump and the rumble of the coaches echoing around the station until with a large hiss from the vacuum brake handle come to a stand as the first of our many passengers join our train.

The down platform here is furnished with a large wooden waiting shelter and the up platform opposite contains the main station building which is constructed of stone in the Brunellian style with tall chimneys and a canopy.

Situated at the Taunton end of the main street in Langport, the station generated a high level of passenger traffic between here and Taunton. A second station – Langport East located on the north side of the town had been open since the Castle Cary cut-off line was opened in 1906.

The large goods yard at Langport West is situated on the up side of the line, and extensive sidings served a weighbridge, goods shed, cattle pens and dock, situated near the up line at the Yeovil end of the platform. A large warehouse, store and coal offices are located further along the yard layout beyond the station forecourt.

Situated near a curve in the river Parrett, the station was often flooded, and all locomotives waded through with their dampers closed, in case water came through the open flap and put the fire out!

Whilst we await the guards whistle - Alec Bowditch now recalls his railway days at the station.

WORKING MEMORIES OF LANGPORT WEST BY ALEC BOWDITCH

'My railway career with the Great Western Railway commenced at Taunton Goods Depot in March 1935. I was 14½ years of age, and had been successful, after an interview with the Goods Agent to obtain employment as a lad messenger. This was in the hungry 30's, and jobs with a future were hard to come by.

I was informed that I was on probation for six months. I overcame the probation period, and my railway career ended 45 years later when redundancy reared its head.

At the age of 20 years I became a member of the RAF during WW11 and was absent from the GWR until almost six years later. I was back in harness by the spring of 1946 and for the following four years was employed as a Porter and then Motor Driver. A good portion of my service life with the RAF was as a driver, and also as a clerk within the M.T. section.

Due to clerical shortages at Taunton Goods Depot I was requested by the Goods Agent to assist with office duties at Taunton. This led me to make an application in 1949 to transfer to the railway clerical office. I sat an examination at the District Office in Exeter that year. However almost a year went by and I was then told to report to the Station Master at Langport West to occupy a vacancy in the Goods Office.

I duly met the Station Master on a Monday morning in September 1950. This was Mr Teague, a softly spoken Devonian who hailed from Bovey Tracey. Prior to Langport West he had been the S.M. at Hemyock. Mr Teague took me to the Goods Office and introduced to the clerical staffs who were as follows: Leslie Blight Chief Clerk, Clarence Elsbury, Fred Burrows, Dennis Chedzoy, and Mike Champion.

It was a busy office, and the six of us were kept fully employed. Under the GWR Zonal Collection & Delivery Scheme (1947) Langport West became a sub depot under Taunton. In turn Langport received goods rated (small's) traffic for both Martock and Somerton.

In railway terminology any traffic passing over a goods shed platform was described as "small's" although, in many instances this was a misnomer, as there were many cumbersome and heavy consignments loaded and unloaded which arrived by through vans from Bristol and Paddington on a daily basis. Likewise rail vans were despatched to these centres combined with traffic from the two out-stations.

A trunk motor service operated from Taunton to Langport also on a daily basis. The Zonal C & D scheme eliminated the station truck working which had operated from late Victorian times.

Travelling daily Monday to Saturday I would catch the 6.52 am train from Taunton (all stations to Yeovil Pen Mill). At Athelney, Clarence Elsbury, Dennis Chedzoy and Mike Champion would join me. Arriving at Langport at about 7.35am. Saturday being a half-day we would return on a train leaving Langport West at around noon.

Staff in the Goods Department at Langport West at that time were, as I recall - Bert Champion, Sid Hector, 'Nobby' Knowles, Charlie Bishop, Jack Merchant. Motor Drivers: Arthur & Bill Champion, Les Riley. Jim Flood would come in from Martock to collect traffic for that area, likewise Dick Woodfield from Somerton.

The daily goods train that served all stations on the branch brought in the goods yard traffic. Traffic for the goods shed was shunted into position, and likewise through truckloads of general goods including coal, placed into sidings in the yard.

General Goods (inwards) consisted of the following; -

Bradford & Sons; - Cement from Snodland, Plaster from Kegworth, Asbestos corrugated sheeting & rainwater goods from Farnworth. Coal & coke.

Edwards; - Agricultural machinery such as – elevators, ploughs and tractors.

Hambridge Brewery; - Wines & Spirits empty barrels and beer crates.

Prideaux's; - Egg trays in railway containers

Pocock & Son; - Coal and Coke

Outwards Yard Traffic; -

Osiers; Bradfords, Grinter Jeanes and Parsons, Langfords.

Teazles; Various farms in the area

Fresh meat in insulated containers from Cobden & Sons Martock

Livestock; Cattle etc loaded from the livestock pens on market days.

A variety of goods were handled for delivery to and from customers in the area, the one major manufacturer was Foxcroft who manufactured travel goods and had premises close by the station. Their products were despatched for destinations nationwide.

The signalmen I can recall in the early 50's were Ted Glanville and Percy Goddard. The one station porter I remember was Fred Lock.

There was a small office building adjacent to the passenger station, and this was the domain of Ted Harvey the P&W Inspector. Langport Goods and Passenger stations were busy places during the 1950s and a happy place in which to work. I can recall that once during my three years at Langport, the line being flooded, this did not impede the station working. Bert Champion, who was in charge of the goods yard working and assisting with shunting, had a pair of thigh waders issued to cope with these conditions.

Being in daily contact by telephone with both Martock and Somerton stations. I recall that at the former - Eddie Russell was the goods clerk and Doris Richards covered the booking office. Harold Tout was a passenger porter at Martock during the 1930/40s; he eventually became a passenger guard at Taunton and then promoted to Platform Inspector until he retired in the 1960's. Harold was a real character with a fund of stories relating to his railway experiences.

Commuters using the passenger trains; - Traffic was quite brisk with people travelling either to Yeovil or Taunton and pupils travelling to St. Gilda's Convent from Bridgwater and Taunton used the train services to and from Langport on a regular basis.

I was moved back to Taunton Goods Depot in 1953 to take up a clerical post of Claims Clerk. And in order to obtain promotion in 1961 was successful in obtaining the post of Claims Investigator at the Divisional Managers office in Bristol. I remained within the railway claims organisation until 1968, later as a Claims Investigator when I became well known to the staff in the Yeovil area'.

Thankyou Alec for giving us an insight into the workings of a busy branch line station.

Meanwhile back on our locomotive, we are ready to go, no need for a single line token as it is double track from now on, well at least until we reach Athelney.

With just a touch on the steam blower, to stop fumes blowing into the cab, the fire is a bright throbbing mass as I turn the injector off, the vacuum brakes are off and the reverser is in full forward gear, heat combines with the smell of hot oil and steam around the cab as I lean out of the cab looking towards the rear of the train.

The last carriage door is slammed shut, the station starting signal arm has already been lowered, at precisely 7.45am departure time, the sound of the guards whistle combined with the sight of his green flag being waved vigorously gives me the moment to shout over to my mate 'right away, ok the road'.

The regulator is opened and with a blast on the whistle we move forward, our locomotive settling down on the axles whilst pulling away underneath the overbridge, exhaust steam and smoke slam under the bridge arch as we pull away from the station.

With the reverser eased back and the regulator opened wider we head towards the Langport West advanced starting signal which is combined with the Curry Rivel Junction down branch distant signal both of the signal arms are lowered giving us a clear road ahead.

The ATC bell rings in the cab as the contact shoe fitted under our locomotive meets the steel ramp between the tracks; we rattle onwards to the junction with all signals in our favour.

We pass the 41 lever Curry Rivel Junction signal box which is standing on our right hand side and situated in the vee created by the Yeovil branch and the West of England main line.

The speed limit for Yeovil trains running through the junction is 25 mph and with a standing start at Langport West, there wouldn't be much chance of us exceeding this limit.

Our locomotive rocks slightly as we cross from the down branch and on to the down West of England main line heading for our next stop, which is three miles away.

This section of line from the junction to Athelney was originally part of the Yeovil branch until it was swallowed up, doubled and upgraded with the opening of the direct route from Castle Cary in 1906.

Time to place a few rounds of coal around the firebox as we bowl along the main line, our speed increasing as the regulator is opened wider, the cab is riding well on the superbly engineered main line, we have ample steam pressure, without lifting our safety valves and thus wasting steam.

My mate is happy and we have time for a bit of banter as exhaust steam beats down on our coaches following on quite happily behind us.

This main line is the haunt of express trains running between Paddington and the West, names such as the legendary *Cornish Rivieria Express* and the *Mayflower* come to mind, the top flight of Western Region steam power including King's and Castle's would be seen on this route.

YEOVIL DUTY No. 521.
4 F.T. (57 XX Class)

—	Yeovil Loco.	5.30 a.m.	‖
5.35 a.m.	Yeovil Pen Mill	6. 0 a.m.	F
6.20 a.m.	Hendford	—	
	F—Shunting 6.25 a.m. to 8.10 a.m.		
	F—Shunting 9.0 a.m. to 11.20 a.m.		
—	Hendford	11.30 a.m.	F
11.35 a.m.	Yeovil Town ...	11.45 a.m.	‖
11.50 a.m.	Pen Mill	12.25 p.m.	V
12.27 p.m.	Yeovil Town ...	12.35 p.m.	‖
12.40 p.m.	Yeovil Loco.	1. 6 p.m.	‖
1.11 p.m.	Hendford	—	
	F—Shunting 1.15 p.m. to 6.0 p.m.		
6.25 p.m.	Yeovil Town ...	6.40 p.m.	F
6.48 p.m.	Yeovil Jc.	7. 0 p.m.	‖
7. 5 p.m.	Yeovil Town ...	7.25 p.m.	F
7.30 p.m.	Pen Mill	7.57 p.m.	F
8. 2 p.m.	Yeovil Town	**	‖
**	Loco. Yard...	—	

5554 drifts cautiously through the floods at Langport West on 29 October 1960.

John Cornelius

A Yeovil-Taunton train arrives alongside the down platform at Langport West headed by 4591 on 12 May 1964.

John Cornelius

Flooding is a fact of life on the Somerset Levels, as a Yeovil bound train headed by 5525 steams on through water stretching as far as the eye can see at Langport West 29 October 1960.

John Cornelius

5525 sends a bow wave of water through the platforms upon arrival with a train from Yeovil on 29 October 1960.   *John Cornelius*

9764 arrives cautiously through the floodwater at Langport West with a Yeovil-Taunton train on 29 October 1964.   *John Cornelius*

The fireman gazes from the cab of 5524 working a Taunton-Yeovil train at Langport West on 29 October 1960, this service is awaiting the arrival of a down train, which is signalled in the background.
John Cornelius

A passengers eye view of floods at Langport West, milk churns await collection on the down platform with its wooden waiting shelter.
R.S.Carpenter

The up platform at Langport West in 1962 with 9732 approaching with a Taunton-Yeovil train, water columns were provided on both platforms. Passengers are also waiting a train for Taunton on the down platform opposite.

Peter Barnfield

9732 simmers away alongside the up platform-starting signal, at Langport West, awaiting the arrival of a Yeovil-Taunton train to clear the single line section from Martock.

Peter Barnfield

Having left the main line at Curry Rivel Junction 3733 heads for Langport West with a Taunton-Yeovil train on 6 June 1960.   *John Cornelius*

A Yeovil toTaunton service hauled by 5503 approaches Curry Rivel Junction on 6 June 1960.

John Cornelius

Going home to Taunton 5554 and brakevan come off the Yeovil branch at Curry Rivel Junction on 18 June 1960.
John Cornelius

A Plymouth-Paddington train headed by 6002 *King William IV* runs past Curry Rivel Junction on 18 June 1960. Yeovil branch tracks converge from the left.
John Cornelius

D806 *Cambrian* heads past Curry Rivel Junction with the down Cornish Riveria Express on
18 June 1960.   *John Cornelius*

D810 *Cockade* heads the up Torbay Express at Curry Rivel Junction on 6 June 1960.

John Cornelius

A down express headed by 7036 *Taunton Castle* passing Curry Rivel Junction on 18 June 1960, Yeovil branch tracks diverging to the right.
John Cornelius

Hall Class 4992 *Crosby Hall* at Curry Rivel Junction with an up express on 18 June 1960.
John Cornelius

John Cornelius

D820 *Grenville* with a down service from Paddington rumbles past Curry Rivel Junction on 6 June 1960.

Castle Class 5069 *Isambard Kingdom Brunel* steams past Curry Rivel Junction with a Paddington – Plymouth express on 6 June 1960.

John Cornelius

ATHELNEY TO TAUNTON

ATHELNEY

The warning siren for the ATC sounds in the cab, and is quickly cancelled by my driver as the yellow arm of the Athelney distant signal standing at caution appears ahead of us.

The regulator is closed, and we coast along, the steam blower turned on slightly to stop a blow back from the firebox into the cab, smoke billows from our chimney as there is no demand on the fire.

Ahead of us the outer and inner home signal arms are already lowered as the station comes into sight, the down platform is furnished with a wooden waiting shelter, plus a wooden station building this is situated at the west end of the down platform. Whilst the up platform is furnished with a wooden waiting shelter.

A small goods yard behind the down platform contained two sidings and a hand operated crane with a lifting capacity of 30cwt, a small goods shed was also provided.

With my mate working the brake into our train we rattle along the platform and come to a halt with a screeching of binding brake blocks, I have the injector singing away and lean out of the cab watching what is happening on the platform behind us.

Platform staff are loading parcels etc into the end luggage van, whilst passengers scurry about either leaving or joining the train.

A glance ahead, shows me that the three arm gantry standing between the two main lines, has the far right hand arm lowered, guiding us on to the branch line to Durston. The other two signal arms are for the down loop and down main.

Athelney Station situated on the Curry Moor was one of the original stations opened with the line between Durston and Yeovil in 1853.

The original layout of a solitary platform served by a single line and a goods loop was vastly altered in 1906 with the upgrading of the line to double track status with its enhancement into the cut off route from Castle Cary, the station was also rebuilt.

The original 14 lever signal box dating from 1881 and situated on the north side of the line adjacent to the level crossing was replaced in 1906 by a 37 lever box erected on the opposite of the track adjacent to the new down main line.

The new all timber signal box opened as Athelney West. Another box (Athelney East) was opened at the eastern end of the layout alongside the up main line, having a short life span the East box closed on 22 November 1908. The West signal box then reverting to 'Athelney'.

Up and down goods loops were installed during the Second World War opening in October 1943.

Athelney signal box closed on 5 April 1986 but has survived, being dismantled and moved to Bishops Bridge on the South Devon Steam Railway, now mounted on a new brick base coming into use on 16 September 1999.

Happily the station building which stood on the down platform has also survived, and has been moved, now in use as accommodation/changing rooms on the sports field in the nearby village of Stoke St. Gregory.

Not all of the Yeovil branch services used the branch line to Durston, as the 9.56am weekday & 12.50pm Saturday ex Yeovil, plus the 9.45am, 12.58 weekday 12.40 Saturday ex Taunton would run direct to and from Athelney via Cogload.

Athelney was only served by local services running between Taunton, Yeovil, Frome, Castle Cary and Langport East.

I am daydreaming away leaning on the cab side, enjoying the sunshine and keeping myself as far away from the heat inside the cab as possible, we are all stoked up with plenty of steam, time to turn the injector off before the familiar sound of the guard's whistle brings me back to life, and we start off again.

We pull away from the platform, and I collect the single line token from its post by the signal box and checking it is the correct one from Athelney to Durston before placing it over the handbrake handle as we rumble over the level crossing, and the bridge carrying the line over the River Tone, followed by the small level crossing used by farmers and horses.

The points guide us off the down main line and we cross over the up main line and take the branch line to Durston, we run alongside the up loop for a short while before swinging away from the main line, our locomotive puffing away with enough fire and steam to keep us going.

My mate has the regulator cracked partly open, and is standing there looking over the side, with his hand near the brake handle as we jog along, cows grazing in the fields alongside the track, remind me of the day whilst firing the 'Durston' shunter, this duty involved a Yeovil crew working a light engine, usually a pannier or 45xx loco, light engine to Castle Cary, shunt wagons in the up yard, and then work a small goods down the main line, shunting at all stations until reaching Athelney, thence across the branch to Durston, shunt and return to Castle Cary to drop off our brakevan and guard, and return light engine to Yeovil.

On this particular day, we had left Durston travelling back to Athelney with just the guard's van behind us, as we ran past Lyng Halt, a large cow appeared, and stood in the middle of the track staring at us, we had no choice but to stop.

My mate and I climbed down and approached the beast, which then wandered off along the track, and stopped again, as soon as we neared the animal, yes, it wandered off again, this went on for a few minutes, with the guard now joining in, as cow and railway staff wandered along the track.

We had to get the cow off the track, if it wandered further, towards the main line at Athelney, it wouldn't stand a chance. Anyway we had a bit of luck, there was a farmers crossing ahead, so with our guard opening the gate, and my mate and I closing in on our quarry, the cow decided that it had seen enough of railwaymen for the day and darted through into the field and safety, with gate closed behind the errant bovine, we in company with our guard, strolled back to the engine which was standing on the branch line and resumed our journey to Athelney. All in a days work.

I have digressed, and we now return to our passenger train. The Durston branch distant signal fixed at caution, appears ahead, and just beyond is the single platform of Lyng Halt and as there are people awaiting us, my mate shuts the regulator, applies the vacuum brake and we coast to a halt alongside the platform.

This unstaffed halt opened on 24 September 1928 serving the nearby villages of East and West Lyng this was a request stop, with intending passengers having to wave down the train for it to stop, and a stop order would often be given to the driver from the staff at either Athelney or Durston stations to set down passengers.

Located in a cutting, with access via a path leading from the north side of the road overbridge on the A361, this was a typical example of late 1920's construction by the GWR where the restraints of economy held sway, that the cheapest possible construction was used in sparsely populated districts, platform size 75ft x 8ft, a 12ft x 7ft shelter of light timber construction was also provided.

Lyng was one of a total of 28 Halts opened by the GWR in 1928 the largest number in one year by the Company since 1905 when 51 Halts of differing sizes were brought into use. During the hours of darkness it was the duty of the guard on the last train at night, to extinguish the oil lamps on the platform.

After a few minutes we are on our way again for the short run to Durston whereupon we arrive under a clear signal from the branch bracket signal with the left hand arm guiding us into the east side of the island platform, the right hand arm could also place us alongside the down main platform, however most services arriving off the branch from Yeovil, Castle Cary or Frome would use the east side of the platform, leaving the west side to stopping services arriving from Bristol.

My mate closes the regulator as we coast in, and I turn on the steam and water valves for the injector, with a quick glance over the side of the cab, down to the waste pipe to see if the injector is picking up and singing away.

The single line now broadens out as sidings appear to our left on the run in, I get ready to surrender the single line token as we near the 71 lever frame signal box which stands off the Bristol end of the down platform.

The signalman leans out of his open window to collect the token, none given back to us, as we will continue on main line tracks from now on towards Taunton.

We coast to a stop at the end of the island platform, time to turn the injector off, and with plenty of fire burning away in the firebox, await our passengers to climb aboard. As with our previous stop at Lyng Halt the platform is on the driver's side of the cab.

All too soon the last of our passengers has climbed aboard, and with the platform starting signal arm lowered, we pull away at our booked time of 8.02am with the points switching us from the branch platform on to the Bristol to Taunton main line.

The station disappears behind us as our last coach follows us on to the main line as we head towards Cogload, there can be no delay in our running to Taunton as the following 6.47 ex Bristol stopper is booked off Bridgwater at 8.01 and Durston at 8.11 and we have a booked stop at Creech St. Michael, unlike the down Bristol train which runs non stop to Taunton from Durston.

We near Cogload under clear signals, the rail layout changes dramatically as we swing south parting company from the up Bristol main line which had been running alongside and now drops below us as we climb up the embankment towards the girder bridge carrying us over the up and down West of England main lines.

The flying junction at Cogload may look impressive from the line side, but the view from the footplate is outstanding as we cross over the girder bridge with its lattice ironwork, and looking to our far right Cogload signal box is seen standing alongside the up Bristol main line.

Once over the bridge we run down the embankment until reaching level ground we find ourselves on a quadruple track main line.

The down Bristol line has now become the down relief and the down West of England line running alongside is now the down main, and alongside that are the up main and relief lines.

A forest of lower quadrant signals control this important location, Cogload Junction situated four miles east of Taunton, was originally constructed as a flat junction with the emergence of the cut-off line from Castle Cary in 1906.

However the growth and acceleration of rail traffic was causing problems with the divergence at the junction between the Bristol and Castle Cary routes. The GWR embarked on a massive reconstruction railway works programme, accomplished under funds provided by the Loans and Guarantee Act of 1929 issued by the government for the relief of unemployment. Avoiding lines were constructed at Westbury and Frome thus clearing the remaining bottlenecks on the direct route to the West.

The most impressive and important alteration took place at Cogload Junction, where the old flat junction was replaced by a flying junction, enabling the down Bristol line to cross over the Castle Cary cut-off lines, the signal box was moved northwards, with the suffix 'Junction' being removed, the track was also quadrupled from here to Norton Fitzwarren station the junction of branch lines to Minehead and Barnstaple. Taunton station was also vastly remodelled.

We are rattling along at a good pace, with increased activity on the main lines beside us as we approach Creech Water troughs with their ribbons of water stretching into the distance.

No. 46003 passing Athelney with the Fawley-Tiverton Junction oil train on 9 June 1978.

John Cornelius

Athelney station looking towards the level crossing on 8 December 1963 with the goods shed, yard and crane behind the down platform. The signals arms on the gantry from left to right read: down loop, down main, Durston branch. *C.L.Caddy*

The wooden station building on the down platform at Athelney, this building has survived and can be found on the playing field at Stoke St. Gregory. *C.L.Caddy*

Signalman John Cornelius looks out from Athelney Signal box in August 1979.

John Cornelius

John Cornelius inside Athelney Signal box 27 March 1985. The signal box has survived and is now at Bishops Bridge on the South Devon Railway.

John Cornelius

The abandoned trackbed of the Durston branch lies to the right as cows pick their way over Cutts Drove occupation crossing at Athelney in 1985.   *John Cornelius*

Farmer Stan Dare on his Ferguson tractor and a cyclist use Cutts Drove crossing at Athelney on 13 July 1985.   *John Cornelius*

Athelney station has long gone in this view taken on 8 May 1979, only the abandoned goods shed remains, lifting barriers have replaced the crossing gates, signal No.35 in foreground.

John Cornelius

The end of an era as signal No.35 and all signals are cut down for scrap, the signal box has closed, and from Monday 7 April 1986 the line as far as Somerton will come under the control of Exeter Power box.

John Cornelius

John Cornelius

50022 *Anson* on a Paddington train passing 45037 on a Paddington-Plymouth relief at Athelney on 28 July 1983.

Lyng Halt looking towards Athelney with the junction in the distance on 31 August 1962.

P.J.Garland Collection

2-6-2T 4174 arrives at Lyng Halt with a Taunton-Langport East train on 2 June 1962.

R.E.Toop

A special stop order to set down passengers at Lyng Halt, given to Yeovil Town Driver Den Norris on
17 September 1963.

Den Norris

A branch train from Yeovil threads its way through the tracks whilst approaching Durston on
31 August 1962.

P.J.Garland Collection

A Yeovil-Taunton branch train weaves its way on to the down Bristol main line at Durston on
31 August 1962.
P.J.Garland Collection

The island platform at Durston as seen from a Yeovil-Taunton train, branch train services would use
either platform face.
P.J.Garland Collection

A Penzance-bound express headed by 5917 *Westminster Hall* runs through Durston station on 2 June 1962. An up train is also signalled as 5563 from Yeovil Town shed lifts her safety valves, before proceeding to Castle Cary via Athelney and Somerton complete with guard and brakevan.

R.E.Toop

R.E.Toop

A down fitted freight hauled by 4932 *Hatherton Hall* runs past Durston station on 2 June 1962.

The original layout at Cogload Junction, tracks from left to right; down Castle Cary, up Castle Cary, down Bristol, up Bristol.

Nicholas Chipchase

View taken from a Yeovil-Taunton train passing over the flyover at Cogload on the down Bristol main line, the up Bristol main line to the right, and Castle Cary lines sweeping under the flyover.

P.J.Garland Collection

The signalman takes a breather looking out of the box window at Cogload on 31 August 1962.

P.J.Garland Collection

Cogload signal box viewed here on 10 June 1963 can now be found at the GWR museum at Coleford in the Forest of Dean.

John Cornelius

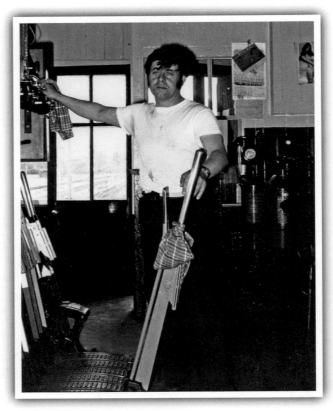

Signalman Maurice Burgess on duty in Cogload signal box.   *John Cornelius*

Viewed from a Yeovil-Taunton train on the down Bristol main line at Cogload, tracks from left to right; up main, up relief, down relief. Plus a Ferguson tractor in the field opposite.

P.J.Garland Collection

Heading a Bristol-Paignton train 5998 *Trevor Hall* at Cogload on 6 August 1961.

John Cornelius

Castle Class 4-6-0 5098 *Clifford Castle* sweeps under Cogload Flyover heading for Castle Cary with the Sunday Perranporth to Paddington express on 6 August 1961.　*John Cornelius*

CREECH WATER TROUGHS TO TAUNTON

The 14 mile long Bridgwater and Taunton canal started in 1823 and completed in 1827 was absolved by the Bristol & Exeter Railway in 1866 for the sum of £66,000 the canal company had by this time seen its fortunes dwindle with the arrival of the railway in Taunton.

The Bristol & Exeter amalgamated with the GWR in 1876 leaving the canal in the hands of a company only vaguely interested in its operation at the time.

The canal from its birth had powers to 'abstract water from any convenient watercourse within 400 yards of the line of the canal' and conveniently the River Tone at a spot just beyond Ham was well within the 400 yard of the line of the canal, for the pumping station to obtain water for the canal.

Up until the turn of the century the GWR used the water in the canal for growing locomotive needs at Taunton Station and also for flushing silt out of Bridgwater Dock.

By contrast in 1901 with the original beam engines of the pumping station nearing their limit with excessive demand placed on them by the railway. The Chief Mechanical Engineer of the GWR George Jackson Churchward authorised the installation of two compound steam engines driving Tangye centrifugal pumps, plus the installation of a new pumping hall at the pump house.

The first water troughs came into on the GWR use at Kenysham in 1895 avoiding the time consuming practice of having locomotives to stop and take on water, in order to speed up its main line services to the West of England running at that time via Bristol.

The water troughs at Creech came into use in February 1902, the location here was ideal, situated on level ground and next to a plentiful supply of water – the Taunton & Bridgwater Canal with water abstracted from the River Tone via the Charlton Pumping Station which had been altered to serve the requirements of the GWR.

Water was pumped into a header storage tank at the pumping station to supply the new troughs which were 18" wide and 6" deep and extended for a quarter of a mile along the up and down main lines.

The pumping and plumbing system was superb, enabling the troughs to refill within three minutes after the passage of a locomotive picking up water. The daily water consumption especially during the busy summer months being approximately 100,000 gallons.

With the Cogload to Norton Fitzwarren quadrupling, the extra tracks at Creech were fitted with water troughs in 1932.

Meanwhile we are forging along on the down relief line past the Charlton Pumping station standing on our left, with water troughs stretching ahead of us on all tracks as we near our final destination, the troughs come to an end and Creech Junction down relief distant signal complete with lowered arm comes into view, the accompanying ring from the ATC bell echoing around the cab

The regulator is shut and we coast along with steam and smoke drifting into the atmosphere, until we stop alongside the 300ft long down platform at Creech St. Michael Halt which was unusual as it was one of the few railway Halts situated alongside a quadruple track main line.

The halt situated 2¾ miles from Taunton opened on 13 August 1928 at a cost of £600, wooden platform shelters were provided on each platform, at this time the main line was double track, however expansion was to come, when the tracks were quadrupled in 1931.

The new layout comprised of two 300ft long platforms, with passengers gaining access to the platforms via footsteps from the adjacent road bridge, the two platforms being equipped with substantial waiting shelters and ticket offices.

The floral displays tended to by staff at the halt were subject to much adulation from passengers and featured in the Great Western Railway Staff Magazine.

Only train services using the up and down main lines could stop here to set down and pick up passengers, all of the signals along the main lines through the halt were controlled by the nearby Creech Junction signal box.

With passengers picked up, the sound of the guards whistle resounding along the platform, clear signals ahead, and with the regulator opened we pull away with a crisp bark from our exhaust, the reverser lever is notched back and we get into our stride for the last part of the journey.

The Chard Branch tracks swing in from our left as we rattle over points and crossovers and run past Creech Junction signal box, main line signals, ringed shunting signals and ground signals abound as we approach Taunton.

Taunton East Junction down relief signal arm is approached at caution, and the ATC siren sounds and is quickly cancelled by my mate as he reads the road ahead of us through the maze of signals and points.

Freight wagons stand alongside us on the goods avoiding lines swinging away to our left, and goods and carriage sidings all over the place, with ex GWR locomotive classes here there and everywhere, main line passenger engines, grimy 28xx freight engines standing in goods loops, shunting pilots fussing about their tasks forming rakes of passenger and freight traffic.

More signals appear ahead, those in our favour guiding us over the myriad of points and crossovers as our coaches' lurch and sway behind our engine.

Taunton East Junction intermediate down relief home signal arm is lowered, but Taunton West Station down relief distant arm which shares the same post stands at caution, immediately the ATC siren sounds in the cab, this is quickly cancelled by my mate.

Taunton West Station down main signals have their arms lowered as we approach the station, more brake application as we run along the down main platform, under light steam with regulator closed, the lovely sound of our vacuum pump slapping away echoing along the platform, countered by the sound from our chimney of the exhaust rising and falling as the vacuum brake is applied and then released again, until finally with a large hiss from the vacuum ejector we coast to a stand alongside the platform at our booked time of 8.14am, one hour nine minutes after leaving Yeovil and stopping at nine stations en route to Taunton.

The fire is just under the firedoor with the injector on to keep the engine quiet, the footplate is swept up and tidy, with the firing shovel standing neatly in the corner of the cab on my side, enough steam on the pressure gauge for any requirements, and the boiler gauge glass tube is showing about three quarters of a glass of water.

The last of our passengers have alighted as platform staff slam shut the open carriage doors and we are now under the control of the shunting staff, as we pull forward under clear signals and run towards and into the carriage sidings, the locomotive yard to our left is full of locomotives, with the usual accompaniment of smoke, steam, and noise.

At the carriage sidings, the shunters are waving us in on the siding selected by them until we are motioned to stop. The shunter has uncoupled us from our coaches; this set will be used on the Barnstaple branch later on in the day before returning to Yeovil.

Taunton was the hub of branch line services radiating to Barnstaple, Chard, Minehead and Yeovil. The station itself covered a large area and comprised four main line and seven bay platforms.

Trains arriving from or departing for the Castle Cary cut-off lines used the island platforms; services to and from Bristol and the North used the outside roads. The down bay (No.2) was used by Chard branch trains in both directions, up arrival bay (No. 8) by trains arriving from Barnstaple & Minehead, down departure bays (Nos. 3 & 4) utilised by departures to Barnstaple and Minehead and certain Exeter stopping trains, up departure bay (No. 9) by Bristol and Yeovil trains.

Although, I was a Southern Region fireman used to the main line between Salisbury and Exeter. Fair play to the 'Western' I was always impressed with Taunton in the steam era, in those days it was a very busy location, with all of the main line services, as well as the local and branch trains bringing track occupation to a maximum at times. And only needed a late running train to bring the timetable into overload.

We have run through the station and take water before reversing into bay 9 and coupling on to the coaches which we will take back to Yeovil on the 9.45am departure, first stop Athelney, running back via the up relief line at Cogload, with a booked arrival at Pen Mill of 10.13am, take water at Yeovil and make a quick can of tea before returning to Taunton with the 11.21am and upon arrival at 12.25pm we are relieved by Taunton men who take our engine to shed, and we walk through the subway and along the up main line platform to bay 9 where we find our engine already coupled to the train, this was usually a pannier or a Standard 2-6-2 tank, there would be no sign of the Taunton crew, we stow our kit away and work back home with the 12.40 to find our relief waiting for us. All in a days work.

The final year for the Yeovil branch came in 1964 with the closure date set for Monday 15 June the final passenger trains running on Saturday 13 June as another branch line passed into history.

Locomotives used on the final passenger trains – 13 June 1964; From Taunton; 06.45-82040, 09.45-82001, 12.58-82040, 14.10-4593, 16.25-31802, 17.55-4131, 20.20-4593.

From Yeovil Pen Mill; 07.05-31802, 09.56-82040, 11.21-82001, 12.37-4593, 16.00-4593, 17.45-82040, 1950-4131.

I did not work on the branch on the last day, being rostered on firing duties elsewhere, but I did return to the branch a week after closure to passenger traffic.

The week after the branch closed to passenger traffic, I was booked to work a civil engineers freight train from Yeovil to Taunton with one of our superb Maunsell Class U 2-6-0 tender engines.

After preparing our locomotive we left Yeovil Loco and set off, tender first, light engine to Yeovil Junction whereupon we were signalled into the up yard and coupled up to our train in the civil engineers siding, this was a huge train of bogie bolsters each one loaded with track panels of rail and concrete sleepers.

After coupling up and climbing back into the cab I noticed the track panels were stacked on each wagon as high as our cab roof, giving an uncomfortable sensation, thinking what if the chains holding the panels on to the bogie bolsters snapped, not worth thinking about the consequences. The whole train was vacuum equipped, and not unfitted, which was a blessing.

When the road was clear we set off back down the double-track branch to Yeovil Town with our long train of bogie bolsters and brake van, rumbling and swaying behind us, as it is downhill to the Town not much steam is required, whereupon on arrival we pull up over the crossover's and when the road is clear, reverse back on to the branch line, the road is pulled off for us, after collecting the single line staff, we set sail for Hendford.

It was a sad moment as we ran along the branch, although everything was still in place, signals, stations, signalboxes etc, there was a forlorn feeling with the reality that passenger trains would use this route no more, and freight to and from Taunton would end soon. When we neared Martock something happened, which has remained with me to this day.

Approaching the Martock down distant signal, our whistle was blown as normal, with the signal arms ahead dropping in our favour, then whilst looking out from the cab I noticed people waving at us from the houses alongside the track, as my mate and I waved back, it dawned upon me that, apart from the daily freight from Taunton, we were the only train that would appear that day, maybe the people thought that we had been removing track from the branch line, anyway we blew the whistle heartily as we neared the level crossing rumbled over and exchanged tokens with the signalman.

The branch was dead; pannier and prairie tanks would no longer cross at Martock and Langport West and as we trundled on to the main line at Curry Rivel Junction the points closed behind us. That was the very last time that I fired a locomotive along the Branch.

At Athelney we ran straight down the main line to Cogload avoiding the branch to Durston, and upon arrival at Taunton ran on to the goods avoiding line at East Junction signal box, and under signals controlled by East Loop signal box stabled our train in the goods sidings, went to the shed to take water and turn on the electric turntable inside the roundhouse. We picked up our guard who made the rest of the journey back to Yeovil on the footplate with us.

We returned via Castle Cary and then tender first to Yeovil Pen Mill on the Weymouth line as the signal boxes at Langport West and Martock had closed, they had only opened for the local goods and ourselves.

The 1960s were a bad time for the railway system of our country with hundreds of railwaymen throughout the country thrown out of work, and thousands of miles of railway track facing demolition.

Amid the traffic choked road system of the 21st Century many branch lines including the Yeovil to Taunton route are sorely missed.

Old Oak Common allocated 5932 *Haydon Hall* approaches Cogload on the up relief line 7 July 1960.
John Cornelius

9F 2-10-0 92249 throws a smoke screen over Creech troughs whilst taking water on 30 July 1960.
John Cornelius

With Charlton pumping station in the background 7014 *Caerhays Castle* takes water from the troughs at Creech on 5 August 1961.   *John Cornelius*

John Cornelius

A rare beast hauling a passenger train, 2-8-0 4708 on the up relief line taking water at Creech troughs.

Castle Class 5001 *Llandovery Castle* in action on the down relief at Creech water troughs on
30 July 1960.

John Cornelius

Grange Class 4-6-0 6803 *Buckleberry Grange* replenishes its water supply on the down relief line near
Taunton on 5 August 1961.

John Cornelius

Passengers and onlookers gather for the opening day at Creech St. Michael Halt on 13 August 1928 showing the then double-track main line, which was quadrupled in 1932. The halt was sparsely equipped with wooden shelters; the tall structure on the left was a windmill powering a pump to drain water from the track.
Jim Cole

The gardens at Creech St. Michael Halt were the subject of much praise in the GWR staff magazine.
Jim Cole

Plenty of custom for the GWR at Creech St. Michael Halt as passengers await the train taking them on a school outing to Weymouth in 1931.

Jim Cole

Creech St. Michael Halt from a Yeovil to Taunton train showing how the quadrupling drastically altered the original layout.

P.J.Garland Collection

The main station buildings situated on the up platform at Creech St. Michael Halt on 31 August 1962.
P.J.Garland Collection

Creech St. Michael Halt as viewed from Yeovil-Taunton train, the signalling was controlled from
Creech Junction signal box.
P.J.Garland Collection

THE BRISTOL & EXETER RAILWAY ARRIVES AT HENDFORD

The Bristol and Exeter Railway broad-gauge line from Durston to the terminus at Hendford on the western outskirts of Yeovil opened to passenger traffic on 1 October 1853 and to goods traffic on 26 October of the same year.

Hendford, described as a quiet leafy glade before the arrival of the railway, was one of the ancient tythings of Yeovil belonging to the Maltravers family - Lord's of the Manor of Yeovil. The first owner, Hugh Maltravers being witness to the royal charter granted by King Henry 1 to the monks at Montacute.

Before the arrival of the railway, Yeovil was well served by stagecoaches with evocative sounding titles such as *Quicksilver*, *Traveller*, and *Telegraph* running from local hostelries such as the Three Choughs, Mermaid & Castle Inn to London, Exeter, Bristol, Bath, Weymouth and Taunton.

The journey to London by 1840 was completed in one day by the '*Traveller*' and '*Royal Mail*', the '*Telegraph*' departed from the Mermaid Inn at 7.30am in 1850 for Salisbury where the passengers continued their journey by train to London from the L&SWR terminus at Milford situated on the south-eastern fringe of the Cathedral City to Bishopstoke (Eastleigh) connecting with services to London, Southampton and Gosport. The direct line from Andover (to Milford) opening in 1857 and from Salisbury to Yeovil on 1 June 1860. A coach from Exeter arrived at the Mermaid at noon on its way to London with arrival at the Bell & Crown, Holborn the following day, with a return arrival at 1.00pm on Tuesdays, Thursdays and Saturdays from London to Exeter.

Whitmarsh's Post Coach after arriving from Taunton set out from the Mermaid at 10.00am on Mondays, Wednesdays & Fridays arriving at the Saracens Head Friday Street, London the following day, arriving at 1.00pm from the capital on Tuesdays, Thursdays and Fridays on its way to Taunton.

Whitmarsh & Co's Wagon also set out from Yeovil at 9.00am on Tuesday, Wednesdays & Saturdays to the Saracens Head taking longer to accomplish its journey, returning the following week on Monday, Wednesday & Fridays. *Woolcotts Wagon* departed from the town on Mondays, Wednesdays and Fridays bound for the Swan Inn situated at Holborn Bridge in London.

The Castle Inn also offered daily services to Bath and Bristol via '*Edwards Omnibus*' and the Three Choughs ran services to Dorchester by the '*Royal Mail*' the service also ran on Sundays. What a marvellous sight it must have been with the arrival of each stage coach, the clattering of hooves, wild eyed, sweating horses, the resounding shrill call from the guard's trumpet, the various liveries of each coach, the coachman muffled in clothing against the vagaries of the weather, shouting and cursing whilst reining in the horses, luggage and passengers sitting on the top of the mud splattered swaying vehicle, whilst the better off folk sat in reasonable comfort inside. The ostlers leading fresh horses out from the stables of the various Inns ready for the changeover, passengers climbing aboard or getting off, luggage being thrown on and off, then without further ado, the mighty coaches rumbled off again with much trumpeting and stamping of hooves.

Sadly the day of the long distance stage coach was to end with the arrival of the railway, however local horse transport was to last for many years, over fifty in fact, with many local hauliers actually benefiting by hauling goods from the railhead to traders within the town and surrounding villages.

Saturday 1 October 1853 was a day of high excitement in Yeovil, with many of the industries and shops being closed in order to give the townspeople a chance to celebrate this very special occasion. The construction of the railway and the station had caused great interest, many towns up and down the land were clamouring to be connected to the railway, but for the town of Yeovil the special day had come at last, to be part of the greatest exponent of the Industrial Revolution…the railway.

In this extract from the *Western Flying Post* we can share that very special event through the reporter's own words of 1853.

OPENING OF THE YEOVIL BRANCH OF THE BRISTOL & EXETER RAILWAY

'The anticipated opening of this long delayed line of railway has been the theme of general conversation in the town and neighbourhood for the last fortnight, and preparations were made to celebrate the event in a becoming manner. The Directors were invited to a public dinner at the Town Hall, and the various manufactories and shops in the town, with a solitary exception, were closed in order to afford to the inhabitants generally an opportunity of participating in the festivity and rejoicing of the day.

About half-past eleven o'clock a procession was formed near the Town Hall, and, headed by the Yeovil Brass band, proceeded in the following order to the Railway Station to meet the Directors. After the band came some of the members of the Yeovil Guardian Friendly Society with banners: the Sergeant at Mace in full uniform: the Portreeve and Burgesses: the Committee of Management: the Commissioners: the Gentry: Manufacturers and Tradesmen of the town and neighbourhood: the members of the various trades, with banners closed the procession.

Arrived at the Railway Station, a shower of rain drove them to seek shelter in the buildings, but the fleeting cloud quickly passed away, and after several false alarms the train was signalled as being in sight, but after waiting some time in eager anticipation, the waggish musicians struck up the enquiring tune 'O dear what can the matter be?' This little episode served to relieve the monotony of the waiting time, and after the exercise of a little more patience, the long-expected train came into sight.

The band played, "See the Conquering Hero Comes" and as soon as the train arrived at the Station, the cheers of the assembled multitudes rent the air. The Chairman and Directors (Bristol & Exeter Railway) on alighting, were received by the Portreeve. Mr Thomas Binford Esq., who addressed them as follows: - "Gentlemen, I am happy to see you: I have no robe of office neither have I a written address: but I brought you that which is far better, thousands of warm hearts and happy faces." To which the Bristol & Exeter Chairman, Mr Buller, replied, "You could not have conferred a greater compliment upon us, or given us a warmer welcome than by bringing the numerous assemblage which we see around us".

The Directors then joined the procession, which returned in the order in which it came to the Mermaid Hotel. Many thousands of persons, including a considerable number of ladies, assembled at and near the Station to witness the arrival of the train.

The dinner was provided in the Town Hall, which was very gaily decorated, with flags: and over the head of the table was placed the word Welcome in large characters, surrounded by a wreath of laurel. The demand for tickets was so great that, long before the hour of dinner arrived, the whole number available had been disposed of: and we heard of some instances in which parties were offered a premium of 100 per cent, for their tickets.   Western Flying Post - Tuesday 4 October 1853.

The public dinner advertised to be held at the Town Hall at 3.00pm on the opening day was the subject to some controversy in the local newspapers especially as the dinner tickets were costing 3s.6d (32½p) and wine tickets 10 shillings (50p) including Champagne and other Wines to be issued for the convenience of those gentlemen who may prefer to sit at the Directors table.

It was obvious that the occasion would be patronised by the gentry and well to do, being well beyond the financial means of the ordinary townspeople. The Western Flying Post became a convenient vehicle for people to place their displeasure, as the following letters inform us:

Dear Sir, - As Saturday will be kept as a general holiday, at least the latter part of it, by all classes, the artisan as well as the manufacturer, the mechanic as well as the gentleman, it will be desirable that all should partake in the festivities of the occasion, and that the demonstration should be made as extensive as numbers or respectability can make it. I beg to suggest through your columns, whether the following plan cannot be carried out. It is obvious that all cannot dine at the Town Hall, for two reasons, first that the hall will not admit them, and secondly, the expense will not suit them. My plan therefore is that a subscription of 1s (10p) each be taken, from those who cannot dine at the town hall, for the purpose of refreshments to be provided at the Goods Shed, or some other suitable place. Such subscriptions to be increased by the voluntary contributions of the affluent: that a procession of all classes be formed to meet the directors at the station, where a suitable address can be read, after which party will repair to a place of refreshment according to the ticket he may hold. I conceive, sir, that two or three practical men with yourself, can have no difficulty in carrying out such a manifestation as this, and that such a demonstration will be more appreciated by the directors, than the best venison and champagne, with the few epicures that such a repast will invite. I leave these remarks with your numerous readers, and am, Sir, yours respectfully. J.S.

Another correspondent signing himself as *"A Constant Subscriber"* suggests a similar plan, with the addition that a meeting of all classes should be held in Ram Park, and a procession organised by the Committee to walk to the station to meet the Directors with an address. Those who dine with the Directors to proceed to the Town Hall and the remaining portion (by permission) be allowed to remain in the Goods Station and enjoy themselves in any way the Committee may think fit. A hogshead or two of beer would be appreciated; every person being allowed a moderate quantity. "If anything be done, let it be done to afford all parties some enjoyment on this interesting occasion."

A *"Subscriber"* has also written a letter embodying similar suggestions. We have no doubt that the Committee will do all that lies in their power to make the demonstration as popular as possible, so that all classes may participate in the rejoicing. But, in order to do this well, the public must subscribe liberally. We shall be happy to receive any amount of shilling subscriptions. - [*Editor. Western Flying Post*]

After being wined and dined and subject to the usual customary speeches etc, the directors of the B&E returned to Taunton on the 6.30pm to Durston. A service of five weekday trains each way was provided from the opening plus two each way on Sundays. The new Yeovil terminus station of the Bristol & Exeter Railway was a single storey building constructed in local stone, the platform was 140ft in length. A locomotive shed and goods shed were also provided.

As with all communities that found themselves connected to the railway, the boost to local trade was enormous with many local firms finding markets for their goods far and wide, with products being imported in from manufacturers in the Midlands and North appearing in the windows of the ever growing variety of local shops. Goods trains brought in vast amounts of timber, salt, and other materials; coal for the local gas works, local industries and households was now conveyed to the town in bulk loads by the railway, horse drawn omnibuses met every passenger train with passenger tickets issued from Yeovil reaching 30,000 during 1855.

The glove making industry in Yeovil had an annual production of gloves increased from 300,000 dozen pairs in 1851 before the arrival of the railway, to an increase of 421,000 in 1856 all exported by rail

Mr Arthur Walkley Bookseller, Newspaper and Advertising Agent for the Bristol & Exeter Railway had a stand at the new station and advertised "*he has made arrangements to supply the town and neighbourhood of Yeovil daily, immediately after the first train from London.*" A plentiful supply of new books was also to be found at Mr Walkley's stand "*immediately on publication. "Orders executed from London at a few hours notice."*

The same erstwhile gentleman was also prepared to receive advertising for the Carriages and Stations of the Bristol & Exeter Railway. "*The Carriages of this Company give Advertisers the advantage of the whole line from London to Plymouth, also the Crediton, Tiverton, Yeovil, Weston super-Mare and Clevedon branches. Terms on application at any of the Book Stalls on the line.*"

Market Trains, which proved to be very popular, were run from Yeovil to Bridgwater on Thursdays leaving at 11.10am, picking up at Martock 11.30am and Langport 11.50am. Incoming Market trains for Yeovil arrived on Fridays picking up at Bridgwater, Taunton, Durston, Athelney, Langport & Martock.

Taunton Market held on Saturdays was also served by a train from Yeovil departing at 11.10am. Single 1st or 2nd class tickets were issued for the Market trains and advertised as being available for the return journey by any train on the day.

An excursion train from Yeovil to the Smithfield Cattle Show on Wednesday 7 December 1853 was advertised as picking up at Martock, Langport, Athelney and Durston. Departing from Yeovil at 7.00am with a return fare at 10 shillings for closed carriages and 16 shillings 1st class. Returning from Paddington the next day at 6.30pm.

By 1856 a total of six passenger trains arrived and departed each weekday, with four on Sundays, in addition to several luggage trains.

Expansion of the railway system in Yeovil occurred three years after the opening of the line from Durston when the GWR opened the 26 mile Wilts, Somerset and Weymouth broad-gauge line from Frome to a station on the north east edge of Yeovil at Pen Mill on 1 September 1856. The Bristol & Exeter lost no time in building a single line connecting spur from Hendford to link up with its broad-gauge allies at Pen Mill this came into use on 2 February 1857 this line passing near to the centre of the town

The third Railway Company, the standard gauge London and South Western Railway was now set to appear in Yeovil from the east. The line from Salisbury constructed by the nominally independent Salisbury & Yeovil Railway under the Act of 21 July 1856 and operated by the LSWR had opened in stages, Salisbury-Gillingham on 2 May 1859, Gillingham to Sherborne 7 May 1860 and finally the section from Sherborne to Yeovil on Friday 1 June 1860.

The new route from Salisbury crossed the GWR Weymouth line by means of an overbridge running alongside before turning west and running parallel to the broad-gauge B&E Hendford-Pen Mill spur from the site of the future Town station to Hendford. The initial services on the new line comprised of four from Salisbury and five from Yeovil.

The Salisbury & Yeovil had agreed with the Bristol & Exeter that its line (S&Y) would terminate at Hendford, and this resulted in the final section of S&Y being constructed as standard-gauge by the B&E for approximately one mile alongside their own permanent way, and the B&E also mixed the gauge in Hendford yard in order to facilitate interchange of freight traffic.

In this extract from the Western Flying Post 1860 regarding the opening of the Salisbury & Yeovil Railway to the Bristol & Exeter station at Hendford. We have an eye witness account of the new line between Hendford and the Bradford Abbas cutting, through which the Salisbury & Yeovil gained direct access to Hendford.

OPENING TO HENDFORD OF THE SALISBURY AND YEOVIL RAILWAY

The opening for traffic of the last section of the above named railway-from Sherborne to Yeovil-took place on Friday last. There was no official demonstration, and the proceedings passed off in an entirely quiet manner. Beyond the influx of an abnormal number of visitors (favoured by the delightful fineness of the weather) there was little to indicate that another branch had been opened of that great railway system of which Yeovil has been so important.

A streamer of flags was thrown across the street at the Choughs Hotel and the omnibuses decked themselves in laburnum. The arrival and departure of trains was witnessed in both towns by numerous persons, who assembled at the railway stations for that purpose, and many availed themselves of the opportunity of paying a first railway visit to their friends.

The congratulations mutually exchanged will, we hope prove a fitting commencement of the friendly intercourse of the two towns, now brought into such close communication. On Thursday evening, Mr Godson, the assistant traffic manager of the South Western Railway, arrived in Yeovil, for the purpose of superintending the necessary arrangements.

On Friday, Messrs G. Pain and R. Hetley of Salisbury (directors) came down by the train reaching Yeovil at 12.33, accompanied by Mr Netman the manager of the Salisbury and Yeovil line and Mr Townsend, solicitor to the Company.

These gentlemen after visiting St, John's Church and taking a stroll about the town lunched together with some of the officials connected with the construction of the line, at the Choughs Hotel. We understand that a handsome repast was as usual, provided by Mrs Bullen, comprising all the delicacies in season and out, of season. The Directors left at about half-past three o'clock. The trains throughout the day were the same as announced on the published tables.

The portion of railway now opened, leaving the Hendford station, which will temporarily be used by the South Western as well as the Bristol and Exeter Company, passes for some distance along the branch connecting the Hendford and Pen Mill stations.

Diverging from thence it crosses by a splendid bridge, the river Yeo. This bridge is an admirable piece of construction, and may be regarded as one of the chief features in connection with the works. It consists of five arches, is 50 feet in span, and of cast iron

The line then joins the Wilts and Somerset, running parallel with it through a deep cutting, it gradually rises, by an ascent of about one in 100, and crosses the Wilts and Somerset line near Clifton by a wrought iron bridge, 50 feet long and consisting of one arch.

After joining the main line to Exeter, and passing through the cutting at Bradford, which from its depth, was one of the most laborious and expensive parts of the undertaking, it runs close by Bradford village, near the church, from the fine tower of which floated on this occasion, a flag, in honour of the day – the only "demonstration" of a "public character" that was anywhere visible.

It then proceeds through a near level country to Sherborne. The gradients from Yeovil to the junction at Bradford, are considerable, but after leaving that point become easy. The scenery presented on the newly opened line is of a most diversified and beautiful character.

A lovely view of the grounds at Newton, the property of G. Harbin, Esq., through which the railway takes a circuit, is presented, and near the point where the South Western and Wilts and Somerset lines meet, one of the best views of the town, with the venerable tower of St. Johns, and the hills surrounding it, is obtained.

On emerging from the Bradford cutting a wide and splendid prospect places itself – an extensive and fertile valley – on the bounds of which are seen the magnificent Park of the Earl of Ilchester at Melbury, and part of the equally magnificent and noble grounds, surrounding Sherborne Castle.

Indeed we scarcely know that any person desiring a short railway trip can select one more picturesque and attractive than that between Yeovil and Sherborne. It is only necessary to add that the works have been carried on in the most expeditious and satisfactory manner, and energy truly indomitable has been displayed by the local manager, Mr. Harrison, and the officials under him.

The contractors, as our readers are aware, are the well-known firm of Messrs Brassey and Co. We congratulate the town upon having become a terminus of another great and influential railway company, which doubtless add to its traffic and importance'. Western

Flying Post – Tuesday 5 June 1860

Yeovil Junction situated close to the village of Stoford and the western extension of the L&SWR to Exeter Queen Street was opened on 19 July 1860 seven weeks after the arrival of the Salisbury & Yeovil at Hendford.

Yeovil Town station the most important and convenient for the local population built as a joint venture between the GWR and LSWR opened on 1 June 1861. Hendford was then relegated to goods traffic, and the original B&E station building used for stabling horses. Passenger trains would not stop at Hendford again for 71 years, until Hendford Halt opened on 2 May 1932.

The handsome and grand façade of the new Town station designed by Sir William Tite (architect of the Royal Exchange and the original Nine Elms Terminus) with its projecting wings and large central gable was designed in the Tudor style and constructed in red brick with creamy ashlar dressings.

Three platforms were provided with two overall roofs containing some 15,000 square feet of glass, supported by iron girders and pillars. Number 1 platform the longest at 400ft was used by GWR services and platforms 2 and 3 by the LSWR all lines and sidings were laid to mixed gauge.

Both railway companies had their respective booking offices, waiting rooms, parcels offices and porter's rooms. The B&E & LSWR had separate departments for all services except for signalling which was under the control of the B&E and subsequently the GWR which eventually absorbed the Bristol & Exeter.

The Town station was not run as a true 'joint' station until 30 March 1882, by which time the broad-gauge had disappeared.

Mr George King Forster was the first station master at Yeovil Town in 1861 for the Bristol & Exeter Railway, and John Henry Pendray station master for the London & South Western Railway. The population of the town at the time being 8,846.

Bristol & Exeter Railway Timetable. 1853

	On Weekdays					On Sundays	
	Class 1 & 2	Class 1.2.3	Exp 1 & 2	Mail 1 & 2	Class 1 & 2	Class 1.2.3.	Class 1 & 2
	A.M.	A.M.	P.M.	P.M.	P.M.	A.M.	P.M.
Yeovil....Dpt	8.20	10.30	12.40	3.10	6.30	6.30	3.00
Martock......	8.38	10.50	12.58	3.28	6.48	6.50	3.18
Langport.....	8.50	11.02	1.10	3.40	7.00	7.02	3.30
Athelney.....	9.00	11.12	1.20	3.50	7.10	7.12	3.40
Durston...Arr	9.05	11.20	1.25	3.55	7.18	7.20	3.45

	On Weekdays					On Sundays	
	Mail 1 & 2	Class 1 & 2	Class 1.2.3	Class 1 & 2	Exp 1 & 2	Class 1 & 2	Class 1.2.3
	A.M.	A.M.	A.M.	P.M.	P.M.	A.M.	P.M.
Durston...Dpt	9.25	11.30	2.10	4.30	9.15	9.20	8.40
Athelney.....	9.30	11.35	2.15	4.35	9.20	9.28	8.48
Langport.....	9.40	11.45	2.25	4.45	9.30	9.40	9.00
Martock......	9.52	11.57	2.37	4.57	9.42	9.50	9.10
Yeovil...Arr	10.10	12.15	2.55	5.15	10.00	10.10	9.30

R.E.Toop

2-6-2T 5548 arrives alongside the up main line platform at Taunton on 24 April 1962 with a Minehead to Yeovil train.

4-6-0 *Dummer Grange* runs through Taunton with an express on the down relief line 27 June 1959. Taunton East Goods Loop signal box is on the far right, with the outline of 6010 *King Charles 1* coming off shed in readiness to work a Minehead to Paddington train.
John Cornelius

28xx 2-8-0 2806 (86E) stands alongside Taunton West Loop signal box amid shed debris of clinker and a discarded ashpan rake.

Alec Swain/Transport Treasury

Lens of Sutton Association

22xx 0-6-0 2213 on carriage shunting duties at Taunton station.

Castle Class 4-6-0 5045 *Earl of Dudley* stands alongside the down relief platform at Taunton.

Lens of Sutton Association

2-6-2T 6157 on carriage shunting duties at the West End of Taunton station 6 April 1962, note the lines of carriages on the sidings.

R.E.Toop

The driver of 6943 *Farnley Hall* takes the chance to oil the straps and rods, the top of the water column can be seen above the tender, plenty of steam, almost ready to go with a Cardiff-Goodrington train on 20 July 1958.   *Alec Swain/Transport Treasury*

1361 Class 0-6-0 Saddle tank No.1362 seen here at Taunton on 4 March 1961 known as the 'Humpty Dumpties' this class of loco was introduced in 1910 by the GWR for dock shunting.   *R.E.Toop*

Pannier Tank 0-6-0 5780 is pictured in the roundhouse at Taunton standing alongside 1362.

Alec Swain/Transport Treasury

An up Bristol train arrives behind 4-6-0 No. 4905 *Barton* Hall at Taunton 20 July 1958.

Alec Swain/Transport Treasury

PASSENGERS MUST
NOT CROSS THE LINE
EXCEPT BY MEANS
OF THE SUBWAY

The locomotive yard at Taunton on 19 October 1963, amongst the line up are three 73xx Class 2-6-0's, one 28xx 2-8-0 No.3834 and Castle Class 5071 *Spitfire.*
John Cornelius

45xx 2-6-2T 4507 leaves Taunton with a Yeovil branch train on 3 September 1960, this was the last Wolverhampton built GWR tank engine to remain in service dating from 1907. *John Cornelius*

A very wet 13 August 1960 and 5001 *Llandovery Castle* runs through Taunton with the down 'Cornishman' *John Cornelius*

Castle 4-6-0 No.5047 *Earl of Dartmouth* alongside the down relief platform at Taunton.

Lens of Sutton Association

Modified Hall 4-6-0 No.7904 *Fountains Hall* conveying through coaches for Newcastle upon Tyne arrives alongside the up main platform at Taunton on 20 July 1958.

Alec Swain/Transport Treasury

John Cornelius

No.8745 from Yeovil Town shed (72C) takes water alongside the up relief platform at Taunton on 30 April 1960.